IMpossible

You can't do it, but it can be done

by Pastor Jim Combs and
Dr. Randy T. Johnson

Special Thanks to
Ian Williams

First Edition, April 2017

Published by:
The River Church
8393 E. Holly Rd.
Holly, MI 48442

Scriptures are taken from the Bible,
English Standard Version (ESV)

THE RIVER CHURCH

Printed in the United States of America

This book is dedicated to
the inmates of the Ohio State Prison System

Love you guys,
Pastor Jim

CONTENTS

A NOTE FROM
THE AUTHOR

I remember as a child coming into the house from a full day of play. I would be filthy. If my mom did not take me right back outside to spray me down with the garden hose, she would tell me to leave my clothes in the laundry room, go straight to the bathtub, and not touch anything. You see, you do not have to wash up before taking a bath.

All too often people try to get "clean" or "straighten out" their life before offering themselves to God. They try to do it on their own. You cannot do it! The Bible says we are like a dog. We throw up and then go back to it. That is sick. Why do we return to our unhealthy ways? How do we get healthy? We cannot do it, but it can be done. You can only get your life in order through the work of Jesus Christ. You need to give your life to Jesus and follow Him. He can and will change you.

2 Corinthians 5:17 says, ***"Therefore, if anyone is in Christ, he is a new creation. The old has passed away; behold, the new has come."***

Jesus is willing to turn your mess into a message. He can make you a new creation. Your motto should be 'out with the old life and in with a new life.'

This book contains 52 lessons that are based on messages Pastor Jim shared with the hundreds of addicts who attend Recovery every Tuesday night. Read a lesson every day for a week. Pray about it. Think about it. Talk to others about it.

You cannot do it on your own. You do not need to do it on your own. Let Jesus come into your life. He will take your life and "throw it back to you better." What looks IMPOSSIBLE will have you saying, "I AM POSSIBLE."

Randy "Doc" Johnson

1

THE ASTERISK

The asterisk (*) is that little innocent looking symbol that can sneak up on us. It is common in the legal world to advertise something "unbelievable" and then throw in a lot of conditions we tend to call small print. Every credit card company uses it to announce a new card that has transfer fees, yearly dues, cash advance fees, and an interest rate increase after the initial phase. Buying a car can have its set of asterisk conditions. I have even found myself ineligible for some promotions due to the asterisk and fine print. It is frustrating. I think it is even wrong at times. I have discovered it is important to know the fine print.

God does not mess with fine print. He offers salvation through Jesus Christ to everyone. John 3:16 says, ***"For God so loved the world, that he gave his only Son, that whoever believes in him should not perish but have eternal life."*** God offers eternal life. There is no asterisk after it. You are eligible. Even more exciting, once we become a child of God, there is no asterisk after our names like the addict, convict, divorcee, race, or gender. We are equal children of God.

To become a child of God is as basic as ABC.

1. Admit

Admit you are a sinner. Romans 3:23 says, *"For all have sinned and fall short of the glory of God."* We have all sinned. It may come in different shapes and sizes, but we have all sinned. The problem is found in Romans 6:23, *"For the wages of sin is death, but the free gift of God is eternal life in Christ Jesus our Lord."* Since we have sinned, we deserve death and even Hell. As soon as we learn what we deserve, God offers a free gift in Christ Jesus. Once we acknowledge our sin, it should be followed by action. Acts 3:19 says, *"Repent therefore, and turn back, that your sins may be blotted out."* We need to repent (change our lifestyle), turn away from sin, and try to live a proper life.

2. Believe

We need to believe in Jesus, God's Son. It is His death, burial, and resurrection that offer us eternal life. He died for us. He covered our sins with His death. He is the only way to Heaven. John 14:6 says, *"Jesus said to him, 'I am the way, and the truth, and the life. No one comes to the Father except through me.'"* Jesus is the only way to the Father (God) and hence Heaven. Acts 4:12 speaks of Jesus, *"And there is salvation in no one else, for there is no other name under heaven given among men by which we must be saved."* It is clear that Jesus is the only way to salvation. Romans 5:8 says, *"But God shows his love for us in that while we were still sinners, Christ died for us."* Jesus knew we were sinners and still died for us. You do not need to get right before coming to Jesus. Come to Him and let Him help you get right. People often think they can somehow earn God's love by living right. Ephesians 2:8-9 makes it clear, *"For by grace you have been saved through faith. And this is not your own doing; it is the gift of God, not a result of works, so that no one may boast."* We are saved by God's grace. It is a gift from God. It is not by our works; however, we should do good works as a thank you to Him. Finally, John 1:11-12 tells about Jesus, *"He came to his own, and his own people did not receive him. But to all who did receive him, who believed in his name, he gave the right to become children of God."* Jesus came to earth, and many people did not accept Him. It is sad. However, whoever does receive Him into their life, He gives the title and position *"child of God."* No asterisk is included.

3. Confess

First, we admit we have sinned and commit to trying to change our ways. Second, we believe that Jesus is God's Son who died for our sins. Although they buried Him, He rose again. He came back to life and now can offer us eternal life. Finally, we need to confess it.

We need to confess our sin to God. 1 John 1:9 says, *"If we confess our sins, he is faithful and just to forgive us our sins and to cleanse us from all unrighteousness."* God will forgive us when we confess our sins. There is no asterisk here either. It does not matter how bad the sin and sins were; He will forgive. Romans 9:9-10 says it so beautifully, *"Because, if you confess with your mouth that Jesus is Lord and believe in your heart that God raised him from the dead, you will be saved. For with the heart one believes and is justified, and with the mouth one confesses and is saved."* There is no fine print here. Confess Jesus as Lord. Believe it in your heart. Be saved. Verse 13 adds, even more, clarity, *"For 'everyone who calls on the name of the Lord will be saved.'"*

When you Admit, Believe, and Confess you become a child of God. No asterisk. No fine print.

Welcome to the family.

Who should you contact now that you want to live for Jesus?

_____

_____

_____

Who should you talk to about Jesus?

_____

_____

_____

2

THE UNDERDOG

My entire life I have been a Detroit Lions' fan. It has been a difficult journey, no Super Bowls, one playoff win, and bad team after bad team. I have tried to pick a new team; the Pittsburg Steelers would be much better. The New England Patriots win, but no, my heart goes out to the woeful Detroit Lions, why? The only thing I can think of is I just love an underdog. You know, that team or person that just does not have a statistical chance. Yup, the one the odds are so stacked against that everyone knows there is no way they win.

So why love the underdog? I guess it is because I have been one since the day I was born. Mom (though an amazing lady) had me when she was fifteen. My dad was struggling since childhood with the addiction to alcohol. I was kicked out of school the first time when I was in the fourth grade; wow, that was a bad day. My mom was told when I was in the eighth grade that I was a nice boy, but I was incapable of learning. Growing up with so much family brokenness, there did not seem to be a chance of escaping the mess. Being surrounded as a child with the world of addiction, betting that I would ever break the chains of all of that would be a fool's wager. I guess because I was such an underdog that I love watching them rise above the rubble. I love watching and hoping they will be victorious. My insides leap when I hear of one who did it!

As much of a Detroit Lions' fan as I am, I have fallen in love with another underdog, those struggling in the addictions world. Some amazing people who have not been given, if you may, a snowballs chance, have captured my heart! The statistics say the addict is in trouble and will not win. Those addicted are told over and over again that it is over for them. Once you have entered into that arena, there is no coming out. Jail time, prison terms, family destruction, tethers, drug testing, no driving, no jobs, loss of trust, and even death are what the addict has to look forward to. It is out of my power to help the Detroit Lions win, but I can make a difference in an addict's life. I have felt that pain and know that worthless feeling it brings.

In I Samuel 17, there is the ultimate underdog story; it is so great - David and Goliath! After the event, the local newspaper must have read something like, "Underdog Comes Away with Huge Victory Over Giant." Nobody gave David a chance that day. His brothers did not believe in him; the odds were slim to none. Even his opposition had no respect for him. This thing was over; it was done. This giant was going to squish him. However, that is not what happened, the Underdog overcomes! I have been so personally inspired by this famous Underdog. He has impacted my life and led me to some major victories in my own life. Reading this story repeatedly when it seemed there was no chance always brought me back to knowing there is always a chance. Discovering that "I could not do it, but it could be done" was huge for me. See, no matter how you look at this story, David did not overcome this giant by himself. Not a chance, he could not do it on his own. This giant was way too big; this giant was way too strong for him. This giant had beaten men much stronger than him. This giant

14

had destroyed many lives before David showed up. There had to have been some help that showed up that day.

There sure was an amazing God who is our help in the time of trouble! Psalm 46:1 says, *"God is our refuge and strength, a very present help in trouble."*

Those battling in addiction are facing a giant; one that calls them out every day, just as Goliath did. That taunts them just as Goliath did. I want the world to know that underdogs can win! David proved that to me. He showed that victory could come to those who should not be able to win. He proved to me that just because they say you cannot, does not mean it is true. He proved to me that giants could come down, no matter how big they are. You may not be able to do it but look at the life of David; it can be done!

See it was the giant who got stoned, not David! Woohoo!

What do you need to do to give your total life to Jesus?

_____
_____
_____

3

HONOR TO HERO

It was in 1980 that the Winter Olympics gave us one of the greatest underdog moments in sports' history. The New York Times said the Russians would easily win the gold medal. They said, "Unless the ice melts..." Russia will win again. Led by coach Herb Brooks, what would forever be known as "The Miracle on Ice," unfolded before the eyes of the world. It was February 22 at the Olympic Center in Lake Placid, New York where it all happened. After being down 3-2 after two periods, the team of amateurs and college athletes representing the U.S. managed to score two goals in the 3rd period and shut out the Russians. Players sobbed with the joy over this amazing 4-3 victory. It made no sense, but it happened, the giant was slain, and the underdog was victorious.

Underdogs can still be victorious. I have heard statistics that seem all over the board, but most appear to say there is less than a five percent chance of an addict being victorious. The mass majority of addicts will continue to use, become incarcerated, or lose their lives. Well, whatever the statistics say, we believe that the underdog can be victorious. David somehow managed to overcome this seemingly impossible task. He was a giant looming out there. He was a giant who had many victims notched in his belt. David would not become one of those. David would teach the world for centuries how it could be done. He would introduce us to simple truths that underdogs could use to help them win.

In the story of David and Goliath, you will not find David as a giant killer. You will find someone who needed a giant killed. Much like the addict, the giant has them. The giants of the addict come in all shapes and sizes, crack, heroine, alcohol, prescriptions drugs, marijuana, and many, many others. These giants are holding some amazing people hostage. Physically and emotionally trapped, the giant is laughing at them as he destroys lives every day. David had one taunting him, but David won! How did it happen? Most people ask, how did he do it, sorry, but he did not. How it happened, that is the question.

First, David showed up to face his giant just by honoring his father and mother. In I Samuel 17:17 we find him pleasing his dad. He was just doing what was asked of him. I am convinced there is tremendous power in the principle of honoring your parents. It looks to me that God has made it a foundational principle for all of us. Proverbs 1:8 says, *"Hear, my son, your father's instruction, and forsake not your mother's teaching."* I am even reminded of Paul quoting one of the Ten Commandments in Ephesians 6:1-3, *"Children, obey your parents in the Lord, for this is right. 'Honor your father and mother' (this is the first commandment with a promise), 'that it may go well with you and that you may live long in the land.'"*

What good advice did you ever receive from your parents?

_____

_____

_____

18

This is a huge first step for the underdog. Now not all, but the mass majority of parents do not want their children overcome and destroyed by addiction. Therefore, simple honoring our parents is the first step for the addict to be victorious. It is a huge part of the process.

I remember sitting in the office; I was in the fourth grade. I was being expelled, yes, kicked out of school. I was waiting for my mom to meet with the principal and pick me up. She walked past me and told me to go to the car. I got in the backseat hoping to stay as far away from her as I could. A few minutes later, she finished being briefed by the principal, and we were on our way home. She never said a word all the way home. We turned down our dirt road and pulled into our gravel driveway. She told me to go downstairs to the basement, and she would meet me there. I just knew that is where my life was going to end. I went downstairs where there was only one piece of furniture, which was an old love seat. I remember sitting down and staring at the concrete floor following the cracks with my eyes and waiting. A few minutes later my mom showed up, and with tears streaming down her face, she told me that I had hurt her worse than anything. Nothing or nobody had ever hurt my mom as her oldest son did that day. She walked back upstairs and left me. My mother had been through more pain in her life than most could endure and now I was at the top of the list. That day my life was changed. I promised myself I would never hurt her like that again. That kept me from making decisions that would destroy my life. That moment of declaration that I would honor her led to many giants being overcome, and it allowed this underdog to win!

Today as a grown man, I look back to that as one of the most defining moments of my life. Mom, I am sorry. I hurt you that day, and I am so blessed that you had the wisdom to let that little boy see your pain. I never wanted to see that again. Thanks, mom!

What advice would you give someone who is starting to use?

_____

_____

_____

What advice is or would your parents give you now?

_____

_____

_____

4

HOSTAGE

I heard a funny joke that terrorists took some lawyers hostage. Their ransom price was $20 million dollars. They threatened to release one lawyer at a time if their demands were not met.

Hostage situations are not necessarily funny. However, they can be odd. There have been cases of people holding someone's dog hostage for a particular ransom or to collect a reward. However, if you google search for cats being held hostage, the only articles are about cats holding their family hostage. If you have had a cat, you might understand.

The Bible records a story that has a hostage twist to it.

1 Kings 2:1-6 records David's parting words of advice to his son Solomon, *"When David's time to die drew near, he commanded Solomon his son, saying, 2 'I am about to go the way of all the earth. Be strong, and show yourself a man, 3 and keep the charge of the LORD your God, walking in his ways and keeping his statutes, his commandments, his rules, and his testimonies, as it is written in the Law of Moses, that you may prosper in all that you do and wherever you turn, 4 that*

the LORD may establish his word that he spoke concerning me, saying, 'If your sons pay close attention to their way, to walk before me in faithfulness with all their heart and with all their soul, you shall not lack a man on the throne of Israel.' Moreover, you also know what Joab the son of Zeruiah did to me, how he dealt with the two commanders of the armies of Israel, Abner the son of Ner, and Amasa the son of Jether, whom he killed, avenging in time of peace for blood that had been shed in war, and putting the blood of war on the belt around his waist and on the sandals on his feet. 6 Act therefore according to your wisdom, but do not let his gray head go down to Sheol in peace.'"

King David (the same David who killed Goliath) did not always do things right. He knew he was on his deathbed. He wanted to give his son Solomon some advice, as he became the next king. His advice is interesting. He points out Joab's past betrayals and how he killed some of their friends. David tells Solomon to have Joab killed.

Why did David not deal with Joab himself? Should he not have killed Joab and let his son start his reign with a clean slate?

David did not think he could kill Joab because Joab had some dirt on him. This same David who slew Goliath had an affair with Bathsheba and even had her husband killed. David had Uriah murdered by asking Joab to put him on the front line of battle and then pull the troops back from him. Joab knew this was David's order. David would have felt as if Joab held him hostage. He felt his hands were cuffed. He could not take action on Joab.

Solomon took the advice and ordered Benaiah to kill Joab (1 Kings 2:29-34). He did and became the new commander of the army.

David was held hostage by the knowledge Joab had. God does not want us to be held hostage to anything.

God wants you to have joy and peace and does not want you to be held hostage by addiction, your past, or your circumstances.

Are you going to let addiction hold you hostage for the rest of your life? _____

_____

_____

_____

If you answered no and wanted to do something about it, there are three steps you need to take right now.

1. Admit you are held hostage. Be honest with yourself. Only 2.5% of addicts will decide not to be a hostage to addiction any longer (that is only about three people out of a room full of 100 people). Alcoholics Anonymous says that only 1 out of 100 will stay clean. Admit that you are not where you need to be.

2. Admit that you are willing to pay the price for what you did. You need to deal with the repercussions of what you have done. You many need to apologize to people. You may need to pay people back. You need to make things right. Sometimes prison is a way to get clean.

3. Admit you cannot do it alone. Press into the church or chapel and Christianity. Christianity is not a lifestyle that was designed to walk alone. We need each other. Let others help. God works within and through the church. Church is a way of life! Do not be held hostage by the enemy! Commit your life to Christ, follow Him, and press into Him at all times. He is our Higher Power.

Break the chains on your heart and mind. Be free.

Who is a good person to help you beat this addiction?

_____

_____

_____

5

THE KEY

One day while walking outside a prison near the Sally Port, Pastor Jim found a key. That may not sound like much. People always find change or junk on the ground, but there was something different about this key. It was a key for handcuffs. Right by the prison was a key that represented freeing someone who was imprisoned.

The Bible also talks about keys.

Luke 11:52 says, *"Woe to you lawyers! For you have taken away the key of knowledge. You did not enter yourselves, and you hindered those who were entering."* The lawyers were teachers of the law. When they refused to accept Jesus as the Messiah, they were missing the key to unlocking the Law and the whole Old Testament. They mislead the people and hence had taken away the key of knowledge. These lawyers selfishly deceived the people or kept them ignorant of the truth. They were unwilling to unlock the truth of the Word.

Revelation 1:18 speaks of another key, *"And the living one. I died, and behold I am alive forevermore, and I have the keys of Death and Hades."* This is the key to eternity. Heaven and Hell are real. Jesus died for our sins, but because of His resurrection, He is called the living one. He is alive. When He conquered death, He took away the keys. He could not be locked in, and He made an escape from the wages of sin for us. We do not need to be contained by death or Hades. We can be free. Jesus came to earth, so we would not have to go to Hell. He died in our place. Not only did He save us from Hell, but He has given His followers Heaven.

The lawyers, lawgivers, selfishly controlled the people. Jesus has a different plan on how we are to live. Jesus can unlock your life and set you free. He modeled and taught what Paul later called the fruit of the Spirit. Galatians 5:22-23 says, *"But the fruit of the Spirit is love, joy, peace, patience, kindness, goodness, faithfulness, gentleness, self-control; against such things there is no law."* These nine traits will change your life and those around you.

Remember, Jesus is the key. He can unlock your life and set you free!

1. Love - Jesus loves you unconditionally. He gave His life for us even when we were sinners. Romans 5:8 says, *"But God shows his love for us in that while we were still sinners, Christ died for us."* Jesus went on the cross, opened up His arms, and said, "I love you this much." He died for you.

2. Joy – Only real joy comes from Jesus. It is not just fun. It is more. It involves purpose and meaning. Nehemiah 8:10 says, *"Then he said to them, 'Go your way. Eat the fat and drink sweet wine and send portions to anyone who has nothing ready, for this day is holy to our Lord. And do not be grieved, for the joy of the LORD is your strength.'"* The men found the

strength to press forward in the joy of the Lord. When you know you are involved in something bigger than yourself, it brings joy. This is part of being successful.

3. Peace – Real peace only comes from God. First, when we give our life to the Lord, we experience peace with God. We are no longer at war with Him. Next, comes peace from God. When everything seems out of control, we can still find peace in Him. Philippians 4:7 says, ***"And the peace of God, which surpasses all understanding, will guard your hearts and your minds in Christ Jesus."***

4. Patience – God's Spirit can give you patience. Barbara Erochina has said, "Some days it is a lot harder to be patient. When we're bringing our concerns to the Lord again and again, we grow tired of waiting. It soon begins to feel like our prayers are falling on deaf ears. Often our desire is to take control and just 'do the best we can;' it is our fleshly reaction to the silence." Practice patience while God has you waiting. There are two ways to wait on God with patience or with frustration, either way; the wait will still be the same. God's timing is perfect.

5. Kindness – The first part of Proverbs 19:22 (NASB) says, ***"What is desirable in a man is his kindness."*** Kindness makes us better looking. It is funny to exchange old high school yearbooks and discuss who was "hot." Often the interaction will lead to disagreement as one says, "If you knew him or her" and then adds how their character has affected how one views them.

6. Goodness – Do more goodness, so that you will not do badness. Take on a positive project. Be careful with idle time.

7. Faithfulness – This means being full of faith. Romans 10:17 says, *"So faith comes from hearing, and hearing through the word of Christ."* Faith is the opposite of Fear. Fear has no hope and brings no trust.

8. Meekness – Strength under control. The Greek word used sparks the image of a majestic horse holding back. It is so powerful, yet focused.

9. Self Control – Temperance we must learn to control our thoughts, words, and actions with God's power

Unlock a brighter future. You cannot do it, but it can be done. The key is Jesus Christ.

What area do you want to work on right now?

_____

_____

_____

How can you do it?

_____

_____

_____

_____

6

NASTY TO VICTORY

I wonder what was going through the guy's mind who first ate a snail. Did he lose a bet? Was it a double dog dare? I do not know, but we call it escargot, and it becomes a sort of fancy French gourmet.

How about the delicacy called caviar? Fish eggs can cost over a $100 for an appetizer. Many people like escargot and caviar. For many, it is an example of turning something nasty into a blessing.

In John chapter 2, Jesus turns something nasty into a blessing and a victory. Verses 1-5 set the stage, *"On the third day there was a wedding at Cana in Galilee, and the mother of Jesus was there. Jesus also was invited to the wedding with his disciples. When the wine ran out, the mother of Jesus said to him, 'They have no wine.' And Jesus said to her, 'Woman, what does this have to do with me? My hour has not yet come.' His mother said to the servants, 'Do whatever he tells you.'"* Jesus was at a wedding. It may have been a relative because when they run out of wine Jesus' mother, Mary takes charge. She tells the servants to do whatever Jesus says. By the way, that is not bad advice for us either.

Verses 6-8 give Jesus' solution, *"Now there were six stone water jars there for the Jewish rites of purification, each holding twenty or thirty gallons. Jesus said to the servants, 'Fill the jars with water.' And they filled them up to the brim. And he said to them, 'Now draw some out and take it to the master of the feast.' So they took it."* Jesus told them to go to the front porch and get the large jars that were used for cleaning up before you entered the house or ate. These things were filthy. However, they obey Him and fill them with water. Anyone watching would have thought this "water" was now nasty. Next, they poured some for the master of the feast. This could be the setting for a very embarrassing start for marriage. Not only had they run out of the water, but also now, they were offering the master of ceremonies something apparently nasty.

Verses 9-10 contain Jesus' first recorded miracle, *"When the master of the feast tasted the water now become wine, and did not know where it came from (though the servants who had drawn the water knew), the master of the feast called the bridegroom and said to him, 'Everyone serves the good wine first, and when people have drunk freely, then the poor wine. But you have kept the good wine until now.'"* The master of the feast loved the wine. It is important to realize that he would not have been drinking like some of the others. He was a sort of designated driver. It was his job to stay sober and be in the right mind to be able to evaluate the ceremony later. He was a key witness to whatever went on. In his sober state, he realized this wine was unique. He points out that many people start with good wine but gradually downgrade knowing no one will notice. However, this wedding was different. The best wine came out at the end. Jesus turned something nasty into a blessing and even a victory.

Jesus is willing to do the same for us. He can take us in our nasty state and turn us into something beautiful. James 4:8 says, *"Draw near to God, and he will draw near to you. Cleanse your hands, you sinners, and purify your hearts, you double-minded."* Jesus is only a prayer away. He wants to make a difference in your life.

2 Corinthians 5:17 says it so well, *"Therefore, if anyone is in Christ, he is a new creation. The old has passed away; behold, the new has come."* In Christ, we are a new creation with a fresh start. He is the miracle worker.

Here are three essential points:

1. God can change "nasty" into victory. You need to draw near to God, and God will draw near to you. God's creation is awesome. It is better than any man-made created things.

2. The image of Christianity is not always as it seems. What do you have to lose? Your life is falling apart. Is this thing you will lose worth saving? You need to let go and let God. Quit riding the fence. Be used by God rather than being used by Satan.

3. Get ready to fight, walk in God's path, and God will place a hedge of protection around you. Satan will use all kinds of things against us, especially our past. You have to fight daily to conquer addiction. The Bible tells us to put on the whole armor of God (Ephesians 6:10-18).

Jesus used the Word of God as a defense against Satan. Live as Christ wants you to live. Remember, with Christ all things are possible. When Christ comes into a person's life, He will change things from nasty into victory. Jesus can turn water into wine.

He can change cigarettes into food on the table, alcohol into clothes for your children, drugs into heat for your house, laziness into time with your family, time in the bar into time at Church, and getting high into being baptized.

What ugliness do you need to get out of your life?

_____

_____

_____

_____

7

TRY + UMPH

Self-proclaimed nicknames generally do not hold, but Cassius Clay (AKA Muhammad Ali) referred to himself as "The Greatest." He was also called "The People's Champion" and "The Louisville Lip." Many of us were astonished as he won 56 fights as he "floated like a butterfly and stung like a bee." Being a Detroiter, I have to acknowledge Joe Louis, and I would be negligent to miss Rocky Marciano. However, Ali holds a place in every boxer's heart as very possibly "The Greatest." His recent death was painful for the whole sport's world. He was a fun, flamboyant champion.

One of my favorite stories about Ali happened when he was on a plane. The flight attendant asked him to fasten his seatbelt. He replied, "Superman does not need a seatbelt." To which she quickly replied, "Superman does not need a plane. Fasten your seatbelt."

We get excited when our favorite athlete succeeds. We somehow feel a connection with them, and it makes us feel like we have won too. The greatest champion of all time is obviously Jesus. He defeated death, the Hell, and the grave. He knocked them out cold! He is the hero. He won, and He did it for us. We can have that connection with Him.

Part of Jesus' battle to becoming the greatest champion ever is recorded in Luke 22:41-42, *"And he withdrew from them about a stone's throw, and knelt down and prayed, saying, 'Father, if you are willing, remove this cup from me. Nevertheless, not my will, but yours, be done.'"* Jesus was and is God. He came to earth and walked among the people for 33 years. He was sinless. Seriously, He never sinned. He was innocent, yet He chose to die for us for our sin. It was quite the ordeal. By Him dying for our sin, it would mean He would take all past sin and even the sin of the future upon Himself. Because of this sin, God could not look upon His Son. Our sin was in the way. For the first and only time in all of eternity, God the Father and God the Son were separated. Jesus knew this was coming. He chose the mission but wished there was a different way. A perfect sacrifice was the only means of restoring man's relationship with God. Therefore, Jesus stepped forward. He willingly gave up His life. He stayed on the cross even though He had the power to leave. He died. Fortunately, the story does not end there. Even though they buried Him, He rose again. He is alive. He defeated death, Hell, and the grave. However, remember, it all started with a choice.

You should take these seven steps if you want to be a champion:

1. Admit you are struggling with whatever you are up against. Jesus knew He had a struggle ahead of Him, and He talked to the Father about it. Sometimes and some days we struggle more than others. Our assignment may be one tough cup to swallow.

2. Put others ahead of yourself. Jesus sought God's will and not His own. He put Himself out there for all of us. He did it for the forgiveness of our sin. When you use drugs they make you feel good (for a while), and others feel bad (long term). When you choose not to use, it makes you feel bad (for awhile), and others feel glad. Victory comes when we begin serving others.

3. Honor God. Jesus says, *"Not my will, but yours, be done."* Jesus just wanted to honor God. You need to honor God. Remember God lives in us. Where are you taking God?

4. Ask for help. An angel helped Jesus. The angel strengthened Him. You have the Spirit of God within you. There is nothing wrong with asking for help. Who is your angel?

5. Get more earnest. Jesus had to fight. He was willing to step forward and battle for us. Try with Umph gives triumph. You need to dig deep and fight hard.

6. Realize it is a winnable battle. Isaiah 54:17 says, *"No weapon that is fashioned against you shall succeed, and you shall refute every tongue that rises against you in judgment. This is the heritage of the servants of the LORD and their vindication from me, declares the LORD."* You can overcome physical battles and the verbal/emotional war that may take place.

7. Celebrate your victory and the victory of others. Jesus knocked out death, Hell, and the grave. We celebrate it every Sunday.

Be a champion for Christ.

What is your battle?

_____

_____

_____

_____

_____

_____

Which steps of the seven do you need to work on?

_____

_____

_____

_____

_____

_____

_____

_____

8

FOCUS FORWARD

Have you ever heard of Harpreet Dev? The BBC News reported that Dev is a unique taxi driver in India. That does not sound impressive until you realize he has been driving backward for over 11 years. He even has a special government license plate allowing him to do this. When he was 19 years old, he was driving outside the city and had car problems. He had no money, no phone, and his car was locked in reverse. So he drove all the way back in reverse. He gained confidence and just kept doing it. He hits speeds of up to 50 MPH. Unfortunately, it has taken its toll on his neck and back, but he likes being unique. The Guinness Book of World Records was not interested because he did not have video proving he only drove in reverse.

I agree with Colin Powell, "Always focus on the front windshield and not the review mirror." It is important to determine our destination and then stay focused. Too often, we are sidetracked by doing things like looking into the rear view mirror. We cannot go forward if we are focusing on the past.

Focusing is not a new problem. There has always been the temptation to chase what is unimportant and miss the big picture.

Being sidetracked is dangerous. 2 Samuel 16:5-11 says, *"When King David came to Bahurim, there came out a man of the family of the house of Saul, whose name was Shimei, the son of Gera, and as he came he cursed continually. And he threw stones at David and at all the servants of King David, and all the people and all the mighty men were on his right hand and on his left. And Shimei said as he cursed, 'Get out, get out, you man of blood, you worthless man! The LORD has avenged on you all the blood of the house of Saul, in whose place you have reigned, and the LORD has given the kingdom into the hand of your son Absalom. See, your evil is on you, for you are a man of blood.' Then Abishai the son of Zeruiah said to the king, 'Why should this dead dog curse my lord the king? Let me go over and take off his head.' But the king said, 'What have I to do with you, you sons of Zeruiah? If he is cursing because the LORD has said to him, 'Curse David,' who then shall say, 'Why have you done so?' And David said to Abishai and to all his servants, 'Behold, my own son seeks my life; how much more now may this Benjaminite! Leave him alone, and let him curse, for the LORD has told him to.'"* There are four key characters in this story: Shimei, Abishai, King David, and his son Absalom. David is losing the kingdom and even part of his family. He is having major problems when Shimei comes along and just adds insult to his injury. Shimei likes kicking him while he is down. Abishai is appalled at Shimei's disrespect and obnoxious behavior. He wants to go after him. David calms him down. He reminds him of their purpose in traveling. He keeps him focused. They do not get sidetracked.

People may not trust you or believe you. It may seem like they want you to fail. They may mock you, ignore you, and even disown you. Do not lose focus. Take one day at a time.

It is important to set a destination, target, or goal and to then focus on what has to be done. Losing focus affects decision making.

1. Focus on the facts. "Using" will cost you all you have worked for. The enemy wants to distract you. You need to be around friends who will be honest with you and help you see the big picture. Side issues can sway you from the big issue. It can make the difference between freedom and incarceration.

2. Do not focus on feelings. Focus on facts. You cannot trust your emotions. They can lead you astray, and you will lose focus. Set goals, dig in, and aim for the prize. Spend time with God. Get involved with church or chapel. You cannot trust your feelings. Prisons are full of people who relied on their emotions.

3. You cannot trust your gut feeling. The Bible contains the facts. It is God's Word. It is the life handbook. Bible can have the acronym of Basic Instructions Before Leaving Earth. God never changes. He is always constant. The only way to survive is to stay focused. God loves you so much that He sent His Son to die for you.

4. Focus on Jesus Christ. Because of the resurrection, He is the only One who has the power to victory. As you strive to stay clean and on task, idle time can be an enemy. Serve Jesus by finding ways to focus on others. Do something nice for someone else today.

"Lack of direction, not lack of time, is the problem. We all have twenty-four hour days." Zig Ziglar

Who is distracting you from moving forward?

_____

_____

_____

_____

What do you need to do?

_____

_____

_____

_____

_____

_____

_____

_____

9

ELEPHANTS AND WHALES OH MY

Johh Saxe (1816-1887) wrote this poem on the famous Indian legend story of six blind men and an elephant.

It was six men of Indostan
To learning much inclined,
Who went to see the Elephant
(Though all of them were blind),
That each by observation
Might satisfy his mind.

The First approach'd the Elephant,
And happening to fall
Against his broad and sturdy side,
At once began to bawl:
"God bless me! but the Elephant
Is very like a wall!"

The Second, feeling of the tusk,
Cried, -"Ho! what have we here
So very round and smooth and sharp?
To me 'tis mighty clear
This wonder of an Elephant
Is very like a spear!"

The Third approached the animal,
And happening to take
The squirming trunk within his hands,
Thus boldly up and spake:
"I see," quoth he, "the Elephant
Is very like a snake!"

The Fourth reached out his eager hand,
And felt about the knee.
"What most this wondrous beast is like
Is mighty plain," quoth he,
"'Tis clear enough the Elephant
Is very like a tree!"

The Fifth, who chanced to touch the ear,
Said: "E'en the blindest man
Can tell what this resembles most;
Deny the fact who can,
This marvel of an Elephant
Is very like a fan!"

The Sixth no sooner had begun
About the beast to grope,
Then, seizing on the swinging tail
That fell within his scope,
"I see," quoth he, "the Elephant
Is very like a rope!"

And so these men of Indostan
Disputed loud and long,
Each in his own opinion
Exceeding stiff and strong,
Though each was partly in the right,
And all were in the wrong!

Sometimes we miss what is going on because we get our focus misguided. We focus on the wrong thing or only part of the picture. FOCUS can be an acronym. As we saw in the last chapter, the F would stand for Facts. We need to focus on the facts not feelings. The O would have us focus on Others. When we focus on others, it takes our minds off our own problems. The C is for Christ. Christ does need to be the center of our focus. He brings meaning, value, and purpose. Finally, the word FOCUS ends with US. We should not think less of ourselves. We should think of ourselves less. Our usual tendency is to be selfish and think of our self first.

Christ brings freedom and power into our lives. He loves us so much that He wants our attention. Jonah struggled with this. The first two verses read, *"Now the word of the LORD came to Jonah the son of Amittai, saying, 'Arise, go to Nineveh, that great city, and call out against it, for their evil has come up before me.'"* God loves people. He wanted to let Jonah be part of His plan. He wanted to see the people of Nineveh saved. However, verse 3 gives Jonah's response, *"But Jonah rose to flee to Tarshish from the presence of the LORD. He went down to Joppa and found a ship going to Tarshish. So he paid the fare and went down into it, to go with them to Tarshish, away from the presence of the LORD."* God called; Jonah fled. God said to go west; Jonah went east. Jonah rebelled. It is part of all of our lives. Romans 3:23 says, *"For all have sinned and fall short of the glory of God."* We have all sinned, and our sin affects others. Jonah got on a ship in the opposite direction. Because of Jonah's sin, there was a storm, and everyone's life on the ship was in danger. In verse 12 Jonah tells them the solution, *"He said to them, 'Pick me up and hurl me into the sea; then the sea will quiet down for you, for I know it is because of me that this great tempest has come upon you.'"* The rest of the story is fantastic. Take some time and read Jonah's adventure in

43

a large fish, his change of heart, and how other people are blessed because of him. People can be hurt or helped by our choices and actions.

There are three things we should learn from Jonah's story:

1. God's first response is love. God sent a storm to get Jonah's attention. Sometimes tough times are allowed by God to get your attention because He loves you. God loves everyone and wants them to live a life of freedom.

2. God does not quit on us. God often waits for us to come to our senses. Jonah owned up that he was the reason for the storm. He was honest with everyone. Have you owned up to the sin in your life? Are you blaming others or circumstances instead of living a victorious life? God met Jonah where he was at. God gave Jonah a second chance. Sometimes we get third, fourth, and fifth chances. The sooner we learn, the better it is for everyone.

3. God uses pictures to point us to the Gospel. The fish swallowed Jonah for three days and three nights, which is a picture of the Gospel when Jesus was in the grave for three days and three nights. He too came out alive. He arose. When you are in trouble, throw yourself into the Gospel. Jesus is the only one who conquered death, Hell, and the grave.

Salvation is the same for everyone and anyone who is willing to receive it. We are rebellious. God's love is given. We give up and realize we are the problem. We accept the Gospel that Jesus died for our sins, was buried, and rose again. Then God gives a new life, a second chance. You have a choice: Either keep rebelling and get death or obey God, focus on Christ, and get the life.

Another acronym for FOCUS can be to Follow One Course Until Successful. Choose to follow The One who can make you successful.

What do you need to do to better follow Jesus?

_____

_____

_____

_____

10

SHAKE A LEG

A nthony Robles chose to succeed no matter what. He was determined. As a senior wrestler at Arizona State University, he was undefeated going 36-0. He became the 125-pound NCAA National Champion by beating the defending champion 7-1 in the finals.

Even though Robles was 96-0 his junior and senior year, won two high school state championships, and was a national champion, his top schools were not interested in him. Iowa, Oklahoma State, and Columbia showed no interest. Maybe they were not interested because he was born with only one leg. Robles stepped up and continually took on larger challenges. He was determined to succeed no matter what.

In Philippians 3:13-14 Paul has this same mindset, *"Brothers, I do not consider that I have made it my own. But one thing I do: forgetting what lies behind and straining forward to what lies ahead, I press on toward the goal for the prize of the upward call of God in Christ Jesus."* This verse seems simple for most people. They forget their dull past and press forward. This is not true with the author. Paul was one who persecuted and even killed Christians. When he went from church to church, he would have met widows and orphans that would have tried to discourage him. He constantly needed to forget the past and press on.

It takes all your energy to forget the past and press forward. The tragedy is that most people are running at half throttle; some are not even in gear. When you act on God's concerns, God will act on your concerns. Here are seven ways from Dr. Luther B. Keith to help you succeed:

1. Respond to your responsibilities. Do what you should do. Do not wait for others to do your job. It may be difficult, but it will be worth it. Galatians 6:4-5 says, **"But let each one test his own work, and then his reason to boast will be in himself alone and not in his neighbor. For each will have to bear his own load."**

2. Forget your failures. Isaiah 43:18 says, **"Remember not the former things, nor consider the things of old."** Do not let the past hold you back. Do not quit by saying, "I tried once and failed." You cannot avoid mistakes, but you can learn from them. How many times have you quit? Do not quit quitting.

3. Master your mind. Your mind is the battlefield. Renew your mind through Christ. Your thoughts will become actions. Discipline yourself unto constructive meditation. 1 Peter 1:13 says, **"Therefore, preparing your minds for action, and being sober-minded, set your hope fully on the grace that will be brought to you at the revelation of Jesus Christ."** Unfortunately, "you cannot do it" becomes a mindset. However, you can do it through Jesus Christ. Philippians 4:13 says, **"I can do all things through him who strengthens me."**

4. Learn to love. Love wins. It is the power that sent Jesus to the cross. It is that love that pushes us forward. It is love that summarizes all of the Old Testament. Matthew 22:36-39 says, *"Teacher, which is the great commandment in the Law?' And he said to him, 'You shall love the Lord your God with all your heart and with all your soul and with all your mind. This is the great and first commandment. And a second is like it: You shall love your neighbor as yourself.'"* You need to love God and love others. It is not an option. It is a command. Learn to love.

5. Conquer criticism. 2 Timothy 4:16 says, *"At my first defense no one came to stand by me, but all deserted me. May it not be charged against them!"* People will let you down. Even godly men let Paul down. Paul learned to press forward. Remember God is with you and believes in you. People may criticize you because they are jealous or just bitter with life. Forgiveness is a great way to conquer criticism.

6. Develop determination. Paul writes in 1 Corinthians 9:24-27, *"Do you not know that in a race all the runners run, but only one receives the prize? So run that you may obtain it. Every athlete exercises self-control in all things. They do it to receive a perishable wreath, but we an imperishable. So I do not run aimlessly; I do not box as one beating the air. But I discipline my body and keep it under control, lest after preaching to others I myself should be disqualified."* Christianity is a marathon and not a sprint. Do not give up. Set your mind on never stopping. Make your walk with God your top priority.

7. Study the Scriptures. Joshua 1:8 says, *"This Book of the Law shall not depart from your mouth, but you shall meditate on*

it day and night, so that you may be careful to do according to all that is written in it. For then you will make your way prosperous, and then you will have good success." Success comes through studying, learning, and living based on the Word of God.

You need to have the mindset to succeed no matter what. You better have a plan for your life – Satan does.

What is your plan?

_____

_____

_____

_____

What do you need to do?

_____

_____

_____

_____

_____

_____

11

ANSWER THE CALL

Brother Andrew is called "God's Smuggler." He started smuggling Bibles into communist countries back in the 1950's. Early on, he was driving into Romania. Every car was stopped, they all had to get out, and take everything out of the car. This happened to the twelve cars in front of Brother Andrew. He was praying. He knew he could not sway anyone, so he even put a few of the hidden Bibles right out in the open on the front passenger seat. His car approached the border guard. He handed him his passport. The guard looked at it, gave it back, and told him to go on. No search, no problem. In 1981, he smuggled one million Bibles into China in one night. He started the ministry named Open Doors.

Brother Andrew once said, "God does not choose people because of their ability, but because of their availability."

God has a plan for your life. It is better than any plan you have had. Are you listening? Are you willing to be available?

Jeremiah had an unusual calling. Jeremiah 1:4-10 says, *"Now the word of the Lord came to me, saying, 'Before I formed you in the womb I knew you, and before you were born I*

consecrated you; I appointed you a prophet to the nations.'
Then I said, 'Ah, Lord God! Behold, I do not know how to
speak, for I am only a youth.' But the Lord said to me, 'Do
not say, 'I am only a youth'; for to all to whom I send you,
you shall go, and whatever I command you, you shall speak.
Do not be afraid of them, for I am with you to deliver you,
declares the Lord.' Then the Lord put out his hand and
touched my mouth. And the Lord said to me, 'Behold, I have
put my words in your mouth. See, I have set you this day
over nations and over kingdoms, to pluck up and to break
down, to destroy and to overthrow, to build and to plant.'"

God knew Jeremiah before he was even born. God already had a
plan for him. Jeremiah tried making excuses, but God comforted
him. God told him not to be afraid because He would give him the
words to say. God has a plan for you, too.

From the start, God had a plan for man and woman. He walked
around the garden with them talking and enjoying creation. He
had a plan and only gave them one restriction. Think about it;
they only had one law. Genesis 3:6-9 records them breaking
that law, **"So when the woman saw that the tree was good**
for food, and that it was a delight to the eyes, and that the
tree was to be desired to make one wise, she took of its fruit
and ate, and she also gave some to her husband who was
with her, and he ate. Then the eyes of both were opened,
and they knew that they were naked. And they sewed fig
leaves together and made themselves loincloths. And they
heard the sound of the Lord God walking in the garden in
the cool of the day, and the man and his wife hid from the
presence of the Lord God among the trees of the garden.
But the Lord God called to the man and said to him, "Where
are you?" Adam and Eve sinned. They messed it up for all of

us. The plan had to be altered. Mankind was now separated from God. Romans 5:12 says, *"Therefore, just as sin came into the world through one man, and death through sin, and so death spread to all men because all sinned."* We are sinners. Fortunately, God still had a plan. He gave His Son. John 3:16 says, *"For God so loved the world, that he gave his only Son, that whoever believes in him should not perish but have eternal life."* God has a plan for us. It is costly. It cost Him His Son. Jesus died for our sins. God can use any of us to do His work. God's plan acknowledges this path:

1. Past – sin is missing the mark of perfection. You need to be sober-minded. You need to make better decisions. Everyone sins. So, what should you do? Be saved. God created a way to cover our sin through Christ's death, burial, and resurrection. Guilt, shame, and death are outside of that mark of perfection. Remember: One out of one people dies.

2. Present – sin hurts others. Sins stop successful living. Learn to hate sin. You need to see it for what it is. You need to change your perspective. Sin wants to control you and even own you. It only offers temporary satisfaction, and the return is empty and negative.

3. Future – live the Spirit-filled life. The Spirit of God lives within Christians. He gives conviction of sin. You need to act upon the prompting of the Spirit.

"God did not direct His call to Isaiah— Isaiah overheard God saying, ". . . who will go for Us?" The call of God is not just for a select few but for everyone. Whether I hear God's call or not depends on the condition of my ears, and exactly what I hear depends upon my spiritual attitude." Oswald Chambers

What is God calling you to do?

_____

_____

_____

_____

What does God want you to do?

_____

_____

_____

_____

12

TRIGGER HAPPY

I have seen some amusing warning signs:

- Warning: Due to the rising cost of ammunition, warning shots will not be fired.
- Prayer is the best way to meet the Lord. Trespassing is faster.
- Attention: Burglars please carry ID so we can identify next of kin.
- This home is protected by the good Lord and a gun. You might meet them both if you show up here not welcome.
- Warning: My alarm tells me you're in my house; my gun tells me not for long.
- Warning: Guns don't kill, proper sight alignment and trigger control do.

In buying a gun, people need to know there are different kinds of triggers. Some triggers are single action only, double action, double action only, double action/single action, and striker-fired or partially cocked striker. Triggers have a big effect on the use of a gun.

Our lives have triggers, too. You need to know the triggers in your life. Good intentions do not keep you clean. Triggers are what set us off. Our tendency when something happens is to think of us first. 1 Corinthians 13 4-7 gives a better reaction in love, *"Love is patient and kind; love does not envy or boast; it is not arrogant or rude. It does not insist on its own way; it is not irritable or resentful; it does not rejoice at wrongdoing, but rejoices with the truth. Love bears all things, believes all things, hopes all things, endures all things."* God is love. His every action is triggered by love. The church at Corinth made a mess of their lives. Yet, God is love. If you pay attention to the concerns of God, God will pay attention to your concerns. In the King James Version, verse 6 says that love is not easily "provoked." What "provokes" or triggers you? If you have the love of God in your life, the effects of those triggers will be less.

There are several triggers in life:

1. Frustration – We do not understand God's love. Frustration can lead us to "use." Frustration can be a trigger. Lean on who God is. Lean on His character.

2. Fear – This is a real life trigger. The enemy plays on your emotions and fears. A great acronym for FEAR is False Evidence Appearing Real. I have heard people say that 90% of the things we fear do not happen or take care of themselves, and the other 10 % we cannot change. So why fear? Philippians 2:6 says, *"Do not be anxious about anything, but in everything by prayer and supplication with thanksgiving let your requests be made known to God."*

3. Feelings – The enemy reminds you of your past. "I don't want to feel therefore I use." Drugs are sometimes used to try to escape

guilt and shame, but they just bring more problems, guilt, and shame. The trigger of feelings commonly occurs when you are on your own. You need to seek God and fellowship with other believers.

4. Friends – If you hang out with pigs, pretty soon you start to smell like a pig. "We have been friends forever." Anyone who encourages you to use is not a friend at all. Friends will hurt you. Love God rather than those so called "friends."

5. Fun – It is fun for a time. It is fake fun. It costs too much. "I deserve to have some fun after what I have been through." Be careful. Some kinds of fun can hurt your family and even have you ending up in jail. If using were not fun, no one would be addicted.

The enemy will try to convince you it is fun and worth it. He wants you to think it is real life. God has a better plan. John10:10 says, ***"The thief comes only to steal and kill and destroy. I came that they may have life and have it abundantly."*** Satan wants to steal your life for his benefit. Jesus wants you to have abundant life. Love is not easily provoked. Love God, live right, and have faith in Him and the triggers in life will be lessened.

What is more important, using or your relationship with God?

_____

_____

_____

13

PRESSURE POINTS

Pressure points can make one feel utterly helpless. I had an uncle who would bend my pinky finger and press in on it. It would put me to my knees. He took real joy in my suffering and could lead me around the room. It was as if I was in bondage.

Acts 12 records a time when Peter was in bondage and felt as if he was totally helpless. Verses 1-5 say, *"About that time Herod the king laid violent hands on some who belonged to the church. He killed James the brother of John with the sword, and when he saw that it pleased the Jews, he proceeded to arrest Peter also. This was during the days of Unleavened Bread. And when he had seized him, he put him in prison, delivering him over to four squads of soldiers to guard him, intending after the Passover to bring him out to the people. So Peter was kept in prison, but earnest prayer for him was made to God by the church."* Peter had guards all around him, yet felt alone. Herod had already killed his friend, James. God did not stop it. Peter had to wonder if his work was finished. I like the last line talking about God's people praying for him. It was earnest prayer.

Verses 6-11 tell the miracle, *"Now when Herod was about to bring him out, on that very night, Peter was sleeping between two soldiers, bound with two chains, and sentries before the door were guarding the prison. And behold, an angel of the Lord stood next to him, and a light shone in the cell. He struck Peter on the side and woke him, saying, 'Get up quickly.' And the chains fell off his hands. And the angel said to him, 'Dress yourself and put on your sandals.' And he did so. And he said to him, 'Wrap your cloak around you and follow me.' And he went out and followed him. He did not know that what was being done by the angel was real, but thought he saw a vision. When they had passed the first and the second guard, they came to the iron gate leading into the city. It opened for them of its accord, and they went out and went along one street, and immediately the angel left him. When Peter came to himself, he said, 'Now I am sure that the Lord has sent his angel and rescued me from the hand of Herod and from all that the Jewish people were expecting.'"* Peter was surrounded by guards and bound with chains. He trusted God to the point that he went to sleep. God sent an angel. The chains fell off. No one else woke up. The angel told him to get dressed and follow him. He passed several guards, and the gates even opened on their own. He was rescued. He was free.

Peter then goes to the house of those praying for him. When he knocked at the door, the servant girl who answered could not believe it was him. She ran to tell those who were praying. They did not believe it was him. He kept knocking and finally they let him in.

In case you do not think to guard Peter was a serious charge, check verses 18-19, *"Now when day came, there was no little disturbance among the soldiers over what had become of Peter. And after Herod searched for him and did not find him, he examined the sentries and ordered that they should be put to death. Then he went down from Judea to Caesarea and spent time there."* That next morning everything looked normal except Peter was gone. His escape cost the guards their life. They failed at an important task.

Peter's rescue and escape were a miracle. Whether your bondage is physical, emotional, or an addiction, there is hope.

There are five points that we need to learn from this event.

1. The angel tells Peter to, "Wake up!" You too need to wake up. Do not spend your entire life in bondage. You were not meant to be in bondage; you were made to be free. Wake up! Do not stay as you are and end up in a state where you one day do not wake up. There are funerals every week of people who stayed the same and refused to wake up.

2. The angel next tells him to, "Get up!" Arise and get dressed. Put your big boy pants on. It is time to grow up. Stop blaming everyone else for your problems. If you are going to be lazy, you better be tough and ready to get run over. God did not create you to be in bondage.

3. Put your shoes on. Get walking on the right path. Be careful with whom you walk. Walk worthy. You are with whom you walk.

4. Put your coat on and prepare for severe weather. Get ready for the world. The enemy wants to keep you in bondage. Quit playing in the world. It wants to destroy you and keep you down. Put your coat on it is rough out there!

5. The angel said, "Follow me." You need to follow the messenger who brings godly advice. You need to listen to what the Bible says. You need to follow Christ.

You need to escape the bondage and grip of the addiction world. Free yourself of the enemy. Jeremiah 29:11 tells you what the Lord has to offer, ***"For I know the plans I have for you, declares the Lord, plans for welfare and not for evil, to give you a future and a hope."***

The church was praying for Peter. God tells us that prayer is the tender nerve that moves the hand of God.

Write out your prayer to God right now.

_____

_____

_____

_____

_____

_____

_____

_____

_____

_____

_____

_____

_____

_____

_____

_____

_____

14

THE REASON FOR THE SEASON

W hat has four legs in the morning, two legs at noon, and three legs in the evening? It is all of us. As a baby we crawled on all fours, then we learned to walk on two legs, and finally, we will probably need a cane meaning three legs. There are different seasons of life.

Ecclesiastes 3:1-8 talks about different seasons or times of life, *"For everything there is a season,*
and a time for every matter under heaven:
a time to be born, and a time to die;
a time to plant, and a time to pluck up what is planted;
a time to kill, and a time to heal;
a time to break down, and a time to build up;
a time to weep, and a time to laugh;
a time to mourn, and a time to dance;
a time to cast away stones, and a time to gather stones together;
a time to embrace, and a time to refrain from embracing;
a time to seek, and a time to lose;
a time to keep, and a time to cast away;
a time to tear, and a time to sew;
a time to keep silence, and a time to speak;

a time to love, and a time to hate;
a time for war, and a time for peace."

There is a different season or time for everything. One of the simple laws in the Bible is that whatever we sow, we will reap. There is a season for sowing, and then there will be a season of reaping. Be careful what you sow. One of the seasons of your life may have been an addiction, and now you are in a season of recovery. If you have not decided to get clean, do not wait any longer. Make today day one. If you are in recovery, congratulations!

There are many seasons of recovery. If you do not understand the seasons of recovery, you will tend to go back. Here are four of the seasons.

1. There is a season of <u>Romance</u>. Maybe you have had the time in your life where you became clean. Maybe you even have a coin commemorating a period of success. That is great. You overcame. Life is new and fresh. It is like a romance. It is exciting.

2. There is a season of <u>Reality</u>. The cravings will still be there. It is a daily battle. Do not get me wrong, God can totally heal you of addiction in the twinkling of an eye, but He generally allows the addict to struggle. It is a daily choice to be clean. There will be emotional turmoil. Memories can look better than they were. Hollywood shows the high and skips the pain of the hangover and the many lives that have been devastated along the way. The tendency is to run back to your first love – drugs, the thrill, the high. You can be hooked emotionally, not just physically. Reality says it will be a battle.

3. There is a season of <u>Regression</u>. In regression, you start acting like an addict. Some respond like an addict even though they are

not using. They choose to live in depression, loneliness, and self-pity. The regression can be physical or emotional.

4. There is a season of <u>Rekindling</u>. You need to renew your relationship with God. You need to be in the Word. You need to pray often. 1 Thessalonians 5:16-18 says, *"Rejoice always, pray without ceasing, give thanks in all circumstances; for this is the will of God in Christ Jesus for you."* You need to constantly have the readiness to pray. Pray should be like a cough; the tendency is always there. In rekindling our relationship with God, we need to realize what James 4:8 says, *"Draw near to God, and he will draw near to you. Cleanse your hands, you sinners, and purify your hearts, you double-minded."* If you are ready to draw near to God, He will draw near to you. You need to realize that if you feel separated from God, it is because you have moved, not Him. He has always been there. It is time for new actions and new thoughts.

Jesus is the Reason for the Season. No matter what season of life or addiction recovery you are in, Jesus is the answer. Look to Him. He can turn your Mess into a Message.

What season of addiction are you in?

_____

_____

_____

_____

How can Jesus help?

_____

_____

_____

_____

15

PROCRASTINA...

People often struggle with procrastination. We put things off. We do not want to inconvenience ourselves right now, so we do not do it. The problem is that when we do not fully handle a project on time, it becomes a bigger problem. Most of us have been told, "A stitch in time saves nine." Taking care of problems immediately saves time, energy, and a lot of trouble in the long run.

Joshua is known as a mighty warrior for the Lord. He was a faithful support man for Moses and then became the leading man. He sought God's will and then led Israel into battle. The command was clear, "Destroy everything, and leave nothing behind." There are times when good enough is not good enough. We need to complete the project 100%.

Joshua 11:21-22 says, *"And Joshua came at that time and cut off the Anakim from the hill country, from Hebron, from Debir, from Anab, and from all the hill country of Judah, and from all the hill country of Israel. Joshua devoted them to destruction with their cities. There was none of the Anakim left in the land of the people of Israel. Only in Gaza, in Gath, and in Ashdod did some remain."*

These verses sound like a success story. Joshua leads Israel into victory. However, it says he left some people in Gath. He almost did everything right.

About four hundred years later in 1 Samuel 17:2-4 we have the battlegrounds set for the historic battle of David and Goliath, *"And Saul and the men of Israel were gathered, and encamped in the Valley of Elah, and drew up in line of battle against the Philistines. And the Philistines stood on the mountain on the one side, and Israel stood on the mountain on the other side, with a valley between them. And there came out from the camp of the Philistines a champion named Goliath of Gath, whose height was six cubits and a span."* You are probably aware of the David and Goliath story. Did you catch where Goliath was raised? He is from Gath. Joshua did not finish his job, and it haunted Israel for hundreds of years.

Joshua did not do what he was supposed to do. If you do not deal with what you need to deal with, it or those things will deal with you. Putting stuff off always costs you more in the long run.

There are at least three things you need to deal with and not put off.

1. Deal with strongholds. Your past can be a stronghold in the addiction world. That stronghold can be what you did and what you were. You need to release that stronghold and move forward as a child of God into victory.

2. Deal with hurt. Addicts often "medicate" to forget hurt. They may excuse their use because someone hurt them. Forgiveness fixes hurts. The enemy's stronghold is also a foothold to try and destroy you. In Christ, your past is gone. Micah 7:19 says,

"He will again have compassion on us; he will tread our iniquities underfoot. You will cast all our sins into the depths of the sea." God threw our sins into the depths of the sea.

3. Deal with guilt. If God has forgiven you, you do not have to feel guilty. Guilt is ugly! Joshua did not deal with Gaza or Gath, and his failure affected many for generations to come. You need to let God have the guilt and its bondage. Make a list of all that you did that you are ashamed of and then realize God took it all. He died for all of them. They were nailed to the cross with Christ. Psalm 103:12 says, *"As far as the east is from the west, so far does he remove our transgressions from us."* Accept God's forgiveness.

Deal with the things that destroy your life. Pull yourself out of the world. Make a change before they destroy you. Jesus gives us the Lord's Prayer in Matthew 6:9-13, *"Pray then like this: 'Our Father in heaven, hallowed be your name. Your kingdom come, your will be done, on earth as it is in heaven. Give us this day our daily bread, and forgive us our debts, as we also have forgiven our debtors. And lead us not into temptation, but deliver us from evil.'"* Check out the last line. Jesus does not encourage them to overcome temptation. He wants them to stay away from it. If you are on a diet, do not open the cookie jar just to see what is inside. You need to think of the people and places that got you into your addiction and avoid them. Change your routine. Relapse is a reality. There are consequences to putting things off. What will it cost you?

If you just keep sweeping problems under the rug, pretty soon you will trip over the rug. I was told growing up that you should check your car oil regularly and change it every 3,000 miles. If you kept putting it off, it could cost you way more. There use to be a commercial that said, "Pay me now or pay me later." Stop procrastinating. Do something positive.

Who do you need to forgive?

_____

_____

Who do you need to apologize to?

_____

_____

16

THE VALLEY OF DECISION

T he Travel Channel came up with a new list of the Seven Wonders of the World:

1. The Great Wall of China. It is about 4,000 miles long.
2. Christ the Redeemer Statue (Rio de Janeiro, Brazil). It is 130 feet tall.
3. Machu Picchu (Peru). It is a granite built city in the mountains.
4. Chichen Itza (Yucatan Peninsula, Mexico). It is a first-century Mayan pyramid.
5. The Roman Colosseum (Rome). It was built in about 75 AD. It seats 50,000, was used for about 500 years, and is still standing.
6. Taj Mahal (Agra, India). It is a white marble mausoleum (tomb) built in the 1600's.
7. Petra (Jordan). It is a city carved into a stone mountain during the time of Jesus.

If I were to add the eighth wonder, it would be the Valley of Decision. Joel 3:14 says, **"Multitudes, multitudes, in the valley of decision! For the day of the Lord is near in the valley of** *decision."* Joel was talking about a place we have all visited. We have times in our lives when everything is going great. We often refer to those as mountaintop experiences; we are King of the Mountain. However, the wonder comes in those times in the valley. It is the Valley of Decision. It is a time of choices. You "wonder" what you should do.

When it comes to who we are and how we are what we are, it comes down to three things.

1. Our genetics have an impact on who we are. Genetics determines eye color, hair color (or lack thereof), height, and even addictions. Yes, even addictions get passed down from parents to children. Exodus 20:5 confirms this, *"You shall not bow down to them or serve them, for I the Lord your God am a jealous God, visiting the iniquity of the fathers on the children to the third and the fourth generation of those who hate me."* You may not be able to choose your past, but you can make a positive difference for future generations.

2. Our environment has an impact on who we are. We can often tell where someone is from by the way they speak. Their accent, slang, and word choice was developed from their environment. When you are thirsty, do you ask for a pop, soda, coke, or carbonated soft drink? I think y'all know what I am talking about. We learned from how we were raised and where we were raised. Maybe you have heard it said, "You can take a boy out of the country, but you cannot take the country out of a boy." The same goes for city folk. We learn from what we see and do. Therefore, be careful with whom you hang out. They will affect you. 1 Corinthians 15:33 says, *"Do not be deceived: 'Bad company ruins good morals.'"* Every excuse has been given for why people use. A common one is that they are a product of their environment.

Okay, then it is time to change.

3. Our choices have an impact on who we are. It is time to stop buying into a con game. It is time to stop making excuses. It is time to make a choice. What will you do? The Bible tells of the time that Joshua was around a lot of people who were making a bad choice. In Joshua 24:15 he said, *"And if it is evil in your eyes to serve the Lord, choose this day whom you will serve, whether the gods your fathers served in the region beyond the River, or the gods of the Amorites in whose land you dwell. But as for me and my house, we will serve the Lord."* Who will you follow? It is a decision that only you can make? The choice is yours. Joshua said he would serve the Lord. No one else can make this decision for you. If they could, you would never use again. Every day you need to make right decisions for your life. Only 1% makes it. Only 1 out of 100 will choose to stay clean and make that choice every day. Right decisions add value to your life, while bad decisions bring pain and devalue your life.

The best choice is to follow Jesus. He has a plan for your life that involves your future and gives you hope. Jeremiah 29:11 says, *"For I know the plans I have for you, declares the Lord, plans for welfare and not for evil, to give you a future and a hope."*

You better have a plan, and it better involve God. You should not be where you are right now. It is your choice. You are in the Valley of Decision.

What will you do? Will you follow Jesus?

_____

_____

_____

17

LEND ME YOUR EARS

I t has always been said or teased that women talk more than men. Louann Brizendine's book, *The Female Brain*, states that women speak about 20,000 words a day while men talk about 7,000. Women speak 13,000 words more than men per day. That is 91,000 words a week. Women speak 4,745,000 more words than men each year. Leo Tolstoy's writing, *War and Peace*, is "only" 560,000 words in English. That is a lot of talking. With that being said, women tend to be better listeners. Women typically talk more and listen better.

At first glance Revelation 3:22 sounds funny, *"He who has an ear, let him hear what the Spirit says to the churches."* It appears to be a form of sarcasm in pointing out that we have an ear and do not use it. Actually, we have two ears. The fact that God gave us two ears and only one mouth might be symbolic for the ratio we should use. Do we listen twice as much as we speak? God asked the Church in Revelation 3 if she is listening. We are the Church, and we need to listen to what the Holy Spirit says.

There are several influences on what we hear. These influences are levels of relationship in which we receive counsel. First, there is the acquaintance. This is our typical brief meeting where someone may say or imply their worldview. Second, is the casual relationship. This is someone we see more often and may stop and open up more. Third, is the close dependable relationship. We go out of our way to talk with this person. Finally, we have the intimate relationship. This is the person we can be vulnerable with, and they will be honest with us. This is the person that must give us godly counsel.

A common phrase I have heard from addicts and inmates is, "I wish I had just listened" or "If I had just listened." You are where you are because of who you listened to and who you ignored.

The organization, Skills You Need, lists ten principles to effective listening: stop talking, prepare yourself to listen, put the speaker at ease, remove distractions, empathize, be patient, avoid personal prejudice, listen to the tone, listen for ideas, and wait and watch for non-verbal communication.
I want to focus on three actions that need to take place to be a better listener.

1. Prepare your ears. The phrase we saw early, *"He who has an ear,"* is found seven times in the Bible (Revelation 2:7, 11, 17, 29; 3:6, 13, 22). Also, the phrase, *"He who has ears,"* is recorded six times (Matthew 11:15; 13:9, 43; Mark 4:9; Luke 8:8; 14:35). Although we have ears, it does not mean we will use them. There is a difference between hearing and listening. You need to prepare your ears and whole self to listen. You learn while listening. It is hard to learn while talking.

2. Prepare your feet. You need to get away from the company of ungodly people. Psalm 1:1 says, *"Blessed is the man who walks not in the counsel of the wicked, nor stands in the way of sinners, nor sits in the seat of scoffers."* Watch where

you go. It is a slippery slope. You start off by just checking out the scene. Next, you just drop in to see what is happening. Finally, you become one of them. It will end up destroying you. Watch where you go.

3. Prepare your heart. Jeremiah 25:4 describes our world today, *"You have neither listened nor inclined your ears to hear, although the Lord persistently sent to you all his servants the prophets."* You need to listen. You get smarter by listening. You should also pause to listen to yourself. Are you making sense? Do you believe what you are saying? Most important, you need to listen to God. God talks to us in the Bible. Spend time every day reading the Bible. Stop and listen to what God is saying. Finally, spend time with someone who cares about you. Spend time with someone who wants you to succeed.

Each day we spend thousands of words trying to connect with others. James 1:19 gives another approach, *"Know this, my beloved brothers: let every person be quick to hear, slow to speak, slow to anger."* He encourages listening. Focus on listening. Not only will you learn more, but it also will keep you calmer and help you control your anger. Too often the more we talk, the louder we get, and then there is full out anger. Nothing good happens next.

Finally, Jesus is the answer. You may wonder how you can find Him, but Romans 10:17 makes it clear, *"So faith comes from hearing, and hearing through the word of Christ."* Find a Church or Chapel that preaches God's Word. Find a pastor or chaplain that loves Jesus and talks about Jesus. Go there and listen to what God says. Today you might say too many words, but nobody will accuse you of listening too much.

18

LOOK TO JESUS!

I n January of 1850, a teenager woke up one Sunday morning and went for a walk. It was snowing so hard that he had to cut his trip short. He went into an open building to warm up by the fire. It was a Church. The preacher could not make it to Church that day because of the snowstorm. A simple town worker decided to preach. He only spoke for about 10 minutes. The text was, *"Look unto me, and be ye saved, all the ends of the earth."* With that simple message, the teenager got saved. That teen was Charles Haddon Spurgeon (Prince of Preachers, The Soul Winner). He is one of the most famous preachers of all time.

Spurgeon was lost. The world controlled him. Ezra knew what it felt like to be controlled by the world. In Ezra 9:8-9 he says, *"But now for a brief moment favor has been shown by the Lord our God, to leave us a remnant and to give us a secure hold within his holy place, that our God may brighten our eyes and grant us a little reviving in our slavery. For we are slaves. Yet our God has not forsaken us in our slavery, but has extended to us his steadfast love before the kings of Persia, to grant us some reviving to set up the house of our God, to repair its ruins, and to give us protection in*

Judea and Jerusalem." They were slaves to Persia. The walls of their city were destroyed. They were just rubble and ashes. They needed to rebuild their city walls and the temple. No walls made them feel like others could own them, and no temple made them feel as if God had left.

Do you feel like a slave? Maybe you are an inmate feeling trapped in a cell, or you are an addict and feel weak, useless, and hopeless. This passage has three points you need to know when you feel in bondage.

1. God did not forsake you. Deuteronomy 31:6 says, *"Be strong and courageous. Do not fear or be in dread of them, for it is the Lord your God who goes with you. He will not leave you or forsake you."* God is with His children. If you are His child, He will never leave you or forsake you. He has not given up on you.

2. God is merciful to you. Lamentations 3:22-23 says, *"The steadfast love of the Lord never ceases; his mercies never come to an end; they are new every morning; great is your faithfulness."* Look for the beauty around you as God's mercy is new every day. You may be where you are so you have time to focus on Jesus. Look to Jesus.

3. God gives revival. He can give you life again. 2 Corinthians 5:17 says, *"Therefore, if anyone is in Christ, he is a new creation. The old has passed away; behold, the new has come."* We are all important. We all have our battles. God is offering new life. Commit your life to a godly lifestyle. When you make the things of God important, God will make your things important to Him.

If you want to have a personal revival with God, there are four steps you can take. First, humble yourself. Get rid of your pride. Second, admit you are the problem. It is your fault you are at the point you are. Third, rise from the rubble and make up your mind to get out of that mess. Christ will bring beauty from the ashes. Decide to turn from that lifestyle from now on. Fourth, do what you are supposed to do. God will honor your choice to do the hard thing and help you rebuild your life out of the rubble and ashes. He will help you repair the trail of desolation you have left behind you.

Put up walls to protect yourself from the enemy. Live a godly life. Repair your life.

Spurgeon's testimony relates even more. During the sermon, the man looked at his only visitor and said, "Young man, you look very miserable." He continued, "and you always will be miserable—miserable in life, and miserable in death - if you don't obey my text; but if you obey now, this moment, you will be saved." The "preacher" then said, "Young man, look to Jesus Christ. Look! Look! Look! You have nothing to do but to look and live." Whether your prison cell is literal or figurative in addictions, many of you can relate to Ezra's description of Israel being slaves and their city has no walls. You are and will be miserable. You need to look to Jesus!

Are you ready for a revival with God?

_____

How will you start the process?

_____
_____
_____

19

THE BANDAGE FOR BONDAGE

Darwin Awards reports this crazy story:

"This guy pushed his motorcycle from the patio into his living room, where he began to clean the engine with some rags and a bowl of gasoline, all in the comfort of his own home. When he finished, he sat on the motorcycle and decided to give his bike a quick start and make sure everything was still OK. Unfortunately, the bike started in gear, and crashed through the glass patio door with him still clinging to the handlebars.

His wife had been working in the kitchen. She came running at the fearful sound, and found him crumpled on the patio, badly cut from the shards of broken glass. She called 911, and the paramedics carried the unfortunate man to the Emergency Room.

Later that afternoon, after many stitches had pulled her husband back together, the wife brought him home and put him to bed. She cleaned up the mess in the living room, and dumped the bowl of gasoline in the toilet.

Shortly thereafter, her husband woke up, lit a cigarette, and went into the bathroom for a much-needed relief break. He sat down and tossed the cigarette into the toilet, which promptly exploded because the wife had not flushed the gasoline away. The explosion blew the man through the bathroom door.

The wife heard a loud explosion and the terrible sound of her husband's screams. She ran into the hall and found her husband lying on the floor with his trousers blown away and burns on his buttocks. The wife again ran to the phone and called for an ambulance.

The same two paramedics were dispatched to the scene. They loaded the husband on the stretcher and began carrying him to the street. One of them asked the wife how the injury had occurred. When she told them, they began laughing so hard that they dropped the stretcher, and broke the guy's collarbone."

Although this story might get you laughing, life can be tough. Life is tough. Exodus 1:14 describes the life of an Israelite in the time of Moses, *"And made their lives bitter with hard service, in mortar and brick, and in all kinds of work in the field. In all their work they ruthlessly made them work as slaves."* They became slaves. They worked hard with no hope in sight. There was nothing they could do. Finally, Exodus 2:23 gives the people's response, *"During those many days the king of Egypt died, and the people of Israel groaned because of their slavery and cried out for help. Their cry for rescue from slavery came up to God."* The people cried out for help. God heard them. God had Moses in place to take action.

In Exodus 8:20 God tells Moses to go to Pharaoh and say two things, *"Then the Lord said to Moses, 'Rise up early in the morning and present yourself to Pharaoh, as he goes out to the water, and say to him, 'Thus says the Lord, 'Let my people go, that they may serve me.'"* First, God wanted the people out of Egypt. Second, God wanted them to serve Him.

Everyone struggles with some kind of bondage. There are three things that are good to realize while you are in bondage.

1. God's people have always struggled with bondage. There are times when you struggle that you feel like you are all alone. People have always struggled. Sometimes your struggles are your own fault, but sometimes it is out of your control. God might be using your struggle to draw you closer to Him or get someone else's attention. There is a reason for our struggles.

2. Bondage leads to ugliness and if left alone always gets worse. Addiction, like bondage, will just get worse. It is a disease that will overcome you.

3. God listens for His people. The Hebrews called out, and God heard them. He even heard them when they were in bondage. Moses came to help and redeem his people. Jesus came to redeem His people. You have to get out of Egypt (the world) before you get out of bondage. Press towards God. God will even hear you while you are in your mess. It does not matter how smart, tough, or clever you are, you cannot get out of bondage unless you get out of the world (Egypt).

In Joshua 24:14 the people are challenged, *"Now therefore fear the Lord and serve him in sincerity and in faithfulness. Put away the gods that your fathers served beyond the River and in Egypt, and serve the Lord."* Joshua does not only tell them to get out of Egypt, but he also insists they get Egypt out of them. He tells them to *"put ways the gods."* This is good, but it also leaves a void. You need to fill the void with God. Joshua goes on to say, *"and serve the Lord."* The void is created and filled. Joshua continues in the next verse, *"And if it is evil in your eyes to serve the Lord, choose this day whom you will serve, whether the gods your fathers served in the region beyond the River, or the gods of the Amorites in whose land you dwell. But as for me and my house, we will serve the Lord."* Joshua challenges them to make a choice. You cannot have it both ways. Get off the fence.

The enemy makes the world look good to us. However, Egypt (the world) is just a con game.

Everyone struggles with some kind of bondage.

Philippians 3:13-14 tells us to get past the past and press on toward the Lord, *"Brothers, I do not consider that I have made it my own. But one thing I do: forgetting what lies behind and straining forward to what lies ahead, I press on toward the goal for the prize of the upward call of God in Christ Jesus."* Jesus is the answer. He brings freedom.

What bondage do you feel?

_____

_____

_____

How will you get out?

_____

_____

_____

_____

_____

20

WHERE'S THE BEEF?

"Where's the beef?" In 1984, an 81-year-old lady (Clara Peller) looked at her sandwich and asked that now famous question. It was a catchy commercial by Wendy's criticizing other competitors in the fast food industry. The catchphrase became so commonplace that it has been used in other settings to evaluate the substance of an idea, event, or product.

The Church has the mega burger problem. We do not focus on the beef. When you get born again, there are benefits. You receive forgiveness, salvation, the Spirit of God, and peace. You receive something called "justification" which means because of Jesus' work on the cross God will treat you "just as if" you never sinned. One more point, your will eventually receive glorification when you enter Heaven in all its glory.

Colossians 3:1-5 gives the ingredients for the Christian life in the form of a sandwich, *"If then you have been raised with Christ, seek the things that are above, where Christ is, seated at the right hand of God. 2 Set your minds on things that are above, not on things that are on earth. 3 For you have died, and your life is hidden with Christ in God. 4 When*

Christ who is your life appears, then you also will appear with him in glory. 5 Put to death therefore what is earthly in you: sexual immorality, impurity, passion, evil desire, and covetousness, which is idolatry." These verses describe the Christian's justification, sanctification, and glorification. Sanctification is a life lived with a mind on godly things. The church needs to teach sanctification. Our culture likes to hear about justification and glorification, but refuses to own up to sanctification.

Verse 1 gives the bottom bun, *"If then you have been raised with Christ."* Being raised with Christ refers to our salvation, justification. The top bun is seen in verse 4, *"Then you also will appear with him in glory."* Obviously, this refers to our glorification. When we just focus on these two elements, it is a lot of fluff. We need to ask, "Where's the beef?" Verse 2 says, *"Set your minds on things that are above."* This is the start of sanctification. You need to think correctly. Verse 5 gives you another patty on that sandwich, *"Put to death therefore what is earthly in you: sexual immorality, impurity, passion, evil desire, and covetousness, which is idolatry."* Christianity needs to be active. You cannot just sit back; you need to get involved.

1. Until an addict lives a sanctified life, he or she will continue to use. You need to set your affections and mind on things above. Philippians 4:8 says, *"Finally, brothers, whatever is true, whatever is honorable, whatever is just, whatever is pure, whatever is lovely, whatever is commendable, if there is any excellence, if there is anything worthy of praise, think about these things."* Think about what you are thinking about.

2. "Stink'n Think'n" can destroy you. Too many addicts say they are not hurting anyone but themselves. That is a lie. Addiction hurts everyone with whom you come into contact. You need to think on things above. Build the beef.

3. You need to get the Word of God in you so it can flow through you. Joshua 1:8 says, *"This Book of the Law shall not depart from your mouth, but you shall meditate on it day and night, so that you may be careful to do according to all that is written in it. For then you will make your way prosperous, and then you will have good success."* The only time the Bible talks about being prosperous is in the context of one meditating on God's Word. You need to bring your brain and body under submission to the Lordship of Christ.

Preacher R.C. Sproul once said, "The Christian life requires hard work. Our sanctification is a process wherein we are coworkers with God. We have the promise of God's assistance in our labor, but His divine help does not annul our responsibility to work" (Philippians 2:12-13). These verses say, *"Therefore, my beloved, as you have always obeyed, so now, not only as in my presence but much more in my absence, work out your own salvation with fear and trembling, for it is God who works in you, both to will and to work for his good pleasure."*

Clara Peller was a manicurist for 35 years. She did not start as an actress until she was 80 years old. However, she will be known for her key role in saying, "Where's the beef?" This is a great reminder that it is not too late to change for what you are known. Fix your eyes on Jesus for salvation and sanctification.

What do you want to be known for?

_____

_____

_____

_____

How do you want to be remembered?

_____

_____

_____

_____

21

GUY ON A PLUS SIGN

Ayoung boy was struggling in school. He was not doing well; he especially struggled in Math. His parents thought it was due to a lack of effort. Even though they did not go to church, they sent him to a Catholic school.

After his first day at school, he came straight home and studied all night, except for a dinner break, without saying a word. This continued for the upcoming weeks. The parents were excited but wondered why such a change. Finally, the quarter had ended, and his report card would show how he was doing. He brought the report card home and had an "A" in Math. Both parents were excited and asked him what had changed. The little boy said his mindset changed on day one at the new school. "When I walked into the lobby, and I saw that guy they had nailed to the plus sign, I knew those people meant business!"

This story is fun, but the addiction world is no laughing matter. It is deadly. Likewise, it is tough being a Christian. Walking the walk and talking the talk of the Christian life are tough. It takes a lot of effort and hard work.

Ephesians 4:17-32 describes the process of a Christian getting rid of his old self and becoming a new man, *"17 Now this I say and testify in the Lord, that you must no longer walk as the Gentiles do, in the futility of their minds. 18 They are darkened in their understanding, alienated from the life of God because of the ignorance that is in them, due to their hardness of heart. 19 They have become callous and have given themselves up to sensuality, greedy to practice every kind of impurity. 20 But that is not the way you learned Christ!— 21 assuming that you have heard about him and were taught in him, as the truth is in Jesus, 22 to put off your old self, which belongs to your former manner of life and is corrupt through deceitful desires, 23 and to be renewed in the spirit of your minds, 24 and to put on the new self, created after the likeness of God in true righteousness and holiness. 25 Therefore, having put away falsehood, let each one of you speak the truth with his neighbor, for we are members one of another. 26 Be angry and do not sin; do not let the sun go down on your anger, 27 and give no opportunity to the devil. 28 Let the thief no longer steal, but rather let him labor, doing honest work with his own hands, so that he may have something to share with anyone in need. 29 Let no corrupting talk come out of your mouths, but only such as is good for building up, as fits the occasion, that it may give grace to those who hear. 30 And do not grieve the Holy Spirit of God, by whom you were sealed for the day of redemption. 31 Let all bitterness and wrath and anger and clamor and slander be put away from you, along with all malice. 32 Be kind to one another, tenderhearted, forgiving one another, as God in Christ forgave you."*

This passage describes three events.

1. You need to get saved. Knowing of Jesus is just the beginning. You need then to walk and follow Jesus. Verses 20 and 21 talk about learning of Christ and finding Him to be the truth.

2. You need to leave your old self. Verse 17 says to stop walking as the Gentiles do. Verse 19 talks about them giving themselves to sin. Verse 22 clearly states it, *"Put off your old self."* Verse 25 continues the thought by putting off all falsehood. Stop lying. Put off your old habits. Verse 28 says stop stealing (this is sounding like the Ten Commandments). Verse 31 becomes specific in saying that part of the old self that is put off includes bitterness, wrath, and anger. When the old man (self) runs your life, the old man will ruin your life.

3. You need to put on your new self. Verse 23 says to be renewed in the Spirit. You are a new person. Verse 24 clearly states it, *"Put on the new self."* Verse 27 points out that the enemy will still be after you, so avoid him and his children. Verse 29 takes the walk to the talk. You need to clean up your language. Encourage others. Verse 30 reminds you that the Holy Spirit is in you. Do not disobey or ignore Him. Verse 32 specifically points out that putting on the new man means being kind, tenderhearted, and forgiving. Act, think, be different, and put on the new man. The Bible says you will know a Christian by his or her fruit. Follow Jesus and be all in.

Walking the walk is tough as a Christian. Jesus challenged Christians to take up their cross daily. Matthew 10:38 says, ***"And whoever does not take his cross and follow me is not worthy of me."*** Luke 9:23 adds the concept of denying self and taking up your cross. ***"And he said to all, 'If anyone would come after me, let him deny himself and take up his cross daily and follow me.'"***

The key to putting off the old self and putting on the new self is looking at the Man on the plus sign. Give your life to Him. Follow Jesus.

What changes do you need to make in your life?

_____

_____

_____

_____

_____

_____

_____

_____

_____

22

BIG HANDS

Have you ever met a professional boxer? Be careful in shaking hands with them. Their hands are huge blocks of stone. I was told as a child that your heart is about the size of your fist. It cannot be true of those guys.

Guinness World Records lists Robert Wadlow (from the USA) as the tallest man ever. It is stated that he had hands that measured 12.75 inches from the wrist to the tip of his middle finger (If his hand in 12 inches long, is not that a foot?). He even wore a size 25 ring.

There is documentation that says Lui Hua of Shanghai, China has larger hands. His left thumb is over 10 inches long, and his index measured close to 12 inches. His situation was unique because he had a condition known as macrodactyly.

Hand size has often been discussed in sports with athletes like Johnny Bench, Michael Jordan, and Julius Erving. I wonder how Samson of the Old Testament would measure up. Samson could run down a fox, carry city gates, and even overturn pillars; however, he had weaknesses.

Judges 14:1 gives the start of years of turmoil for Samson, *"Samson went down to Timnah, and at Timnah he saw one of the daughters of the Philistines."* Samson had no good reason for going to the "lost people." He was supposed to find a wife from God's people. He wanted to have control of his own life. He wanted to do it his way. God called him for a mighty purpose, and he walked away from it.

Judges 16:30 records his final act, *"And Samson said, 'Let me die with the Philistines.' Then he bowed with all his strength, and the house fell upon the lords and upon all the people who were in it. So the dead whom he killed at his death were more than those whom he had killed during his life."* Finally, he got to the point that he realized he needed God. He cried out to God. God had never given up on him. God heard him and empowered him.

There are three ideas to note about the downfalls of Samson.

1. Samson was hanging out with the wrong people. You cannot trust the wrong crowd. When you are with the wrong crowd, you do some dumb things. Be with the right people.

2. A female sidetracked Samson. The opposite gender in the addiction world can be very dangerous. People do crazy things when they are in love. Addicts need to avoid vulnerable situations. Realize men are either motivators or manipulators.

3. Samson got bad or no advice. You need to listen to good advice. Seek godly advice. Samson went off on his own and did not listen to his parents. He did not have any friends or influences that would challenge him or speak into his life. Remember: God is not done with you yet.

Just receiving counsel is not enough. You need to receive godly, honest advice that is not biased or selfish. In 1 Kings 12, Rehoboam ignores godly advice and accepts what he wants to hear, ***"But he abandoned the counsel that the old men gave him and took counsel with the young men who had grown up with him and stood before him. And he said to them, 'What do you advise that we answer this people who have said to me, 'Lighten the yoke that your father put on us?' And the young men who had grown up with him said to him, 'Thus shall you speak to this people who said to you, 'Your father made our yoke heavy, but you lighten it for us,' thus shall you say to them, 'My little finger is thicker than my father's thighs. And now, whereas my father laid on you a heavy yoke, I will add to your yoke. My father disciplined you with whips, but I will discipline you with scorpions.'"*** Rehoboam had a chance to be a blessing to the people, yet he decided to think of himself based on the advice of people who only thought of themselves. By the way, his analogy of his little finger being larger than someone's thigh sure should put him in the Guinness World Records.

Clint Eastwood said, "A man got's to know his weakness." Everyone has weaknesses, but they do not have to take you down.

Who are you spending your time with?

_____

Do you have someone who will give you healthy wise advice?

_____

Do you give godly advice to others?

_____

23

THE DREAM

The Chinese Bamboo Tree is fascinating. Once it is planted, you need to fertilize it and water it regularly. For the first five years, you will not see any growth. However, after five years it grows ninety feet in just six weeks (about two feet per day). Some have grown as much as one hundred and fifty feet tall.

If you want to grow a Chinese Bamboo Tree you need patience and perseverance. If you want success in life, you need patience and perseverance. You cannot quit. It may take years of looking like it is not working, but you have to keep pressing forward. You cannot even mess up one day. No one else may see or acknowledge growth, but you keep keeping on.

Ecclesiastes 5:3 says, *"For a dream comes with much business, and a fool's voice with many words."* Most people dream of a better life for themselves. Of course, as an addict you know you want a better life. It has to get better. The author of Ecclesiastes says that fools are full of talk and no action. Winners know dreams come with much business. It takes hard work.

In Numbers chapter 13 Moses is leading the people of Israel. They come to the land of Canaan. God tells them it is great land

and that He will give it to them. So, in verse 17 we see what they do, *"Moses sent them to spy out the land of Canaan and said to them, 'Go up into the Negeb and go up into the hill country.'"* Moses sent out twelve spies to check out the land God told them about.

The spies are gone for forty days. They see that the land is great, *"And they told him, 'We came to the land to which you sent us. It flows with milk and honey, and this is its fruit'"* (verse 27). The land is perfect. They all agree. Everything sounds good, but verse 28 starts with the word "however." Dreams are not accomplished with excuses. The verse says, *"However, the people who dwell in the land are strong, and the cities are fortified and very large. And besides, we saw the descendants of Anak there."* Losers see obstacles; winners see opportunities. Ten of the twelve spies lost the dream.

Fortunately, two of the spies pressed toke a stand. Joshua and Caleb said, *"Only do not rebel against the Lord. And do not fear the people of the land, for they are bread for us. Their protection is removed from them, and the Lord is with us; do not fear them"* (Numbers 14:9). You need to remember God is with you. Ten men did not want to go. They did not want to pay the price. Only two were willing to pay the price. They knew the dream would take work. They were willing to step away from the other ten. Sometimes we have to pay the price and not hang out with certain people or go to certain places.

There are three things you need to remember in working toward your dreams.

1. Life can get better. There are awesome things out there for us. God still has a great plan for your life; however, so does the

devil. God loves you and wants to see you succeed; Satan only loves himself, hates you, and wants to see you fail. Every action you make either makes God smile or the devil. Fight forward and see dreams come true.

2. You need to stop rebelling against God. You will not win. Joshua and Caleb were different and wanted to go. The other ten disagreed with them and even wanted to stone them. They wanted to kill Joshua and Caleb. That did not stop those two. They stood strong. The ten never got to see the Promised Land, but Joshua and Caleb did. Ten rebelled against God and lost. Two obeyed God and won. They got to experience the dream.

3. Going back cannot be an option. The past is full of pain and suffering. Sometimes when we dream big, the obstacles get in the way of our thinking. We feel it is too much. The tendency can be to get lazy and want to go back to the old ways. We forget how bad it was. We get in a rut. The ten spies wanted to go back to Egypt. They were slaves in Egypt. It was horrible. They hated it. They did not want to pay the price. They lost their dream. Two knew they needed to press on to the Promised Land. Addiction kills everything. Do not go back to all the pain and suffering you experienced and you caused for others. You need to dream and get down to business.

Did you know that Albert Einstein's parents thought he was dumb? He performed so badly in all high school courses (except math) that a teacher asked him to drop out. A teacher asked Albert Einstein to quit? Yes, but he had a dream and got down to business.

What is your dream?

_____

_____

_____

_____

_____

What will be your first step in the right direction?

_____

_____

_____

_____

_____

_____

_____

_____

_____

24

LIGHT ME UP

L ight can be a very interesting topic. Light travels 186,000 miles per second. So, light that we see from the sun left the sun ten minutes before we see it. It keeps moving until redirected or slowed down by filters. Water is a filter, but sunlight can reach a depth of about 260 feet in the ocean. Light can be a difficult science lesson. However, it can be funny, too.

Did you know about 25% of all people sneeze when exposed to bright light? No, they are not allergic to light. They seem to be affected by a so-called "photic sneeze reflex." It is a condition you are born with that causes you to sneeze when you are hit with bright light. Scientists have studied this all the way back to Aristotle and do not have the answer. It is funny how light can affect us.

Jesus makes a bold statement in John 8:12, *"Again Jesus spoke to them, saying, 'I am the light of the world. Whoever follows me will not walk in darkness, but will have the light of life.'"* The world is full of darkness. It is full of evil and hatred. It is a dead end. Evil men hide in the darkness. They are secretive and selfish. Jesus brings light.

Jesus includes us in Matthew 5:14, *"You are the light of the world. A city set on a hill cannot be hidden."* He says we too are the light of the world. In Galatians 3:26 He says how this happens, *"For in Christ Jesus you are all sons of God, through faith."* Jesus is the Light of the World. When we become followers of Jesus, we become Christians. Christian means Christ-like or little christs. Therefore, we are lights of the world. You are a "mini-me" of Jesus. You are to be a light in this dark world.

You probably hear a voice saying, "You are not good enough." You need to listen to God. You can strive to obtain goodness, but it only comes by God's grace. Then we are good enough. Satan will always remind you of your past and failures. God says you are complete in Him. To whom will you listen?

Jesus will lead you into completeness. His Word is a lamp to our feet and light to our path. He helps us today and for the future. Jesus is all we need. He is enough even when we feel not good enough. Even when we fall, Jesus does not condemn us. Jesus is the answer to all of our insecurities, hurts, sins, failures, ...etc.

There are three things about light that we need to do.

1. We should shine. Since we are the light of the world, we should shine. We should have faith in Jesus Christ and shine. We shine because we have "The Light of the World" in us. His light seeps out. Light shines. That is what it does.

2. We should conquer. When asking if anything can separate us from God's love, Paul writes, *"No, in all these things we are more than conquerors through him who loved us"* (Romans 8:37). When light hits darkness, it wins. Light conquers. A single match can light up a room that was totally dark. No matter how dark the location, it just takes a little light to change it.

3. We should grow. Light cause growth in plants and trees. We should grow because of "The Light" (Jesus). We need to listen to the Word of God. God gives us promises.

Remember Jeremiah 29:11, *"For I know the plans I have for you, declares the LORD, plans for welfare and not for evil, to give you a future and a hope."* Jesus has a plan for you. It is good. It includes a future. It gives hope.

Some might sneeze when touched by the light, but Christians strive to deflect the light of Jesus. God sheds the light of love on us, and we reflect that love to others. God loves us, so we love others. God is good to us, and we are good to others.

Is your present life known for light or darkness?

_____

_____

_____

_____

_____

_____

25

GET GOOD ADVICE FROM YOURSELF?

A guy is not feeling well, so he goes to the doctor. The doctor examines him, leaves the room, and comes back with three different bottles of pills. He tells the man to take the first pill every morning with a large glass of water, take the second pill at lunch with a large glass of water, and take the third pill in the evening with a large glass of water. The man is concerned about how serious his condition is that he needs three kinds of pills every day. He hesitantly asks what the problem is. The doctor says, "You are dehydrated. You are not drinking enough water."

Although the answer seemed pretty simple, at least he did consult someone else. He did seek help. There are three pretty basic things all of us need to do when we are faced with a problem.

1. Consult with God.

Our starting point should always be God. John 18:10 records Peter's reaction when he was faced with a difficult situation, *"Then Simon Peter, having a sword, drew it and struck the high priest's servant and cut off his right ear (The servant's name was Malchus)."* Jesus was going to be arrested, so Peter thought he needed to do something. He drew a sword and tried to kill a guy. He was with Jesus and did not even ask Him what he should do. You need to consult with God, so you do not act in a negative way but choose a positive response.

Even when you want to do something right, you should seek God to make sure it is done in the right way at the right time. In 1 Chronicles 13 David wants to return the ark of God. He wants to do a good thing. Verses 1 says, *"David consulted with the commanders of thousands and of hundreds, with every leader."* David did seek advice from others but should have sought out God first. Unfortunately, due to David's decision, a man died. You need to do the right thing, in the right way, and at the right time. You have some decisions to make, consult God. God will never tell you to get drunk or high. You need to ask, "God, what do you want me to do?" Remember, God is smarter than you.

2. Consult with yourself.

This might sound funny, but ask yourself, "If I was asked for my opinion, what would I say?" You are a smart person. In Psalm 139 we are even reminded that you are fearfully and wonderfully made by God Himself. Think of the consequences of your actions. Nehemiah was faced with a difficult situation. Most of the men were at war, and other men were taking advantage of the women and children. Nehemiah is furious and says, *"I took counsel with myself, and I brought charges against the nobles and the officials. I said to them, 'You are exacting interest, each from his brother.' And I held a great assembly against them"* (Nehemiah 5:7). Nehemiah paused and consulted himself. He then knew what to do. You need to read the Bible so God can tell you what to say to others when they seek your advice, and so you know even what to say to yourself.

3. Consult with people of wisdom.

Finally, it is nice to get advice from others. David was king. After him, his son, Solomon was king. It was common for a son to be the next king. The question became who would be king after Solomon. Would the people follow Rehoboam or Jeroboam? 1 Kings 12 records Rehoboam seeking advice on how to get the people to follow him as king.

Rehoboam first asks the older men their help, and they say, *"Your father made our yoke heavy. Now therefore lighten the hard service of your father and his heavy yoke on us, and we will serve you"* (verse 4). Solomon built the temple. It was expensive, so he taxed the people big time. The older advisors encourage Rehoboam to lighten up on taxes. It seems like this has always been a political issue. Verses 10-11 record the advice his friends gave him, *"And the young men who had grown up with him said to him, 'Thus shall you speak to this people who said to you, 'Your father made our yoke heavy, but you lighten it for us,' thus shall you say to them, 'My little finger is thicker than my father's thighs. And now, whereas my father laid on you a heavy yoke, I will add to your yoke. My father disciplined you with whips, but I will discipline you with scorpions.'"* Rehoboam friends gave bad advice. It was probably even selfish advice as the entourage always celebrates with the leading man. The kingdom split as people withdrew from him.

You need to consult with godly people. Do not just go to people who will always agree with you. Seek truth. Seek good godly advice. Taking advice from another addict can be a mistake. Consult with people who have a godly mindset and want you to succeed.

What advice would you give a friend who is going through what you are going through?

_____

_____

_____

_____

_____

_____

26

RED HERRING

W hen I was young, I was told I was hyper, too active, and lacked discipline. Now, I find out I am ADHD. ADHD stands for Attention Deficit – hey look there is a squirrel. I mean Attention Deficit Hyperactivity Disorder. Professionals say I struggle with focus.

It is interesting how we use animals as a reference for something else. We can refer to people as wise as an owl, strong as an ox, or just say, "She is a fox." Recently, I saw a reference to a "red herring." It appears the red herring symbolizes an unimportant distraction. People who opposed hunting would put smoked herring (smelly fish) across the path to distract or draw the hounds away from tracking the fox. Therefore, a red herring is a distraction.

This relates to you because it is hard for an addict to keep focus. When addicts lose focus, they use.

It is important to look at Ecclesiastes 5:3 again, *"For a dream comes with much business, and a fool's voice with many words."* For a dream to become a reality takes a lot of focus. You cannot get distracted along the way.

Attitude is everything. Remember these two points.

1. If you think you cannot, you probably cannot and will not. Attitude is everything. There is a man in the Bible who said he would not believe Jesus rose from the dead unless he saw and touched him for himself. He became known as Doubting Thomas. Earlier, in John 11:16 we find Thomas already being cynical, *"So Thomas, called the Twin, said to his fellow disciples, 'Let us also go, that we may die with him.'"* Thomas believes Jesus is getting ready to take a trip that will be dangerous. At first he sounds brave by wanting to go along, but actually, he is negative. He had been following Jesus for some time and had a definite dream. Now he is speaking of dying with Jesus. He lost his dream.

Is this happening to you? Have you set goals and do not feel like you are getting anywhere? Does it seem like no one else believes in your dream? The tendency is to quit. The standard response is to stop fighting. The result is getting swallowed up by the world.

2. If you think you can, you probably can and will. Attitude is everything. There is another man from the Bible who continually pressed forward. His name was Paul. In Philippians 4:13 he said, *"I can do all things through him who strengthens me."* The amazing thing about this statement is that Paul was in jail when he said it. He had a dream that he knew was from God. He knew God would give him the strength to do it. He stayed focus. He did not get sidetracked. He later got out of jail but did not stop preaching the Good News of Jesus Christ. He kept his focus.

What is your dream? Have you set goals? If you fall are you willing to get back up? Are you ready to fight forward? Remember, followers of Jesus Christ have God within them. He will direct you. He will give you strength. You can do all things through Him because He will strengthen you.

Proverbs 23:7 (King James Version) adds, *"For as he thinketh in his heart, so is he: Eat and drink, saith he to thee; but his heart is not with thee."* This says you are how you think. If you think negative, negative things tend to happen. However, when you think positive, positive things show up. Some might call it a self-fulfilling prophecy. Our belief affects our behavior.

Take the attitude that you will beat the addiction. Stop using. Stop drinking. Stop going to the dope house. Do not let these things become a "red herring" or distraction from keeping you from being your best. Make your dream a reality and get to work. You will be better and so will those around you.

Do you think you will beat addiction? How?

_____

_____

_____

_____

_____

_____

_____

_____

27

REVOLVING DOOR

Vertigo is a sensation that makes one feel dizzy. It is an inner ear problem that makes one feel like the world is spinning around them. It is the feeling of being off balance. I think it would be funny to see a revolving door at a vertigo center. I mean, would they ever get out? Sorry, I know vertigo is a serious condition. Having proper balance in life is important, too.

HistoryToday records an amazing event that happened in 1859. On June 30th Jean-François Gravelet, nicknamed 'Blondin,' crossed Niagara Falls on a tightrope. The rope was over 1,000 feet long, and it took him 17 minutes to do it. Obviously, the key is to have great balance (and probably be a little bit crazy).

Drugs, alcohol, and all addictions throw one off balance. It is all they can think about. They not only lose their perspective, but also their job, car, house, family, and possibly even life. Balance is vital.

Job was an amazing man. As a matter of fact, Job 1:1 says, *"There was a man in the land of Uz whose name was Job, and that man was blameless and upright, one who feared God and turned away from evil."* He was blameless, upright, and feared God. He was a really good guy. Verse 8 even adds God saying, *"Have you considered my servant Job, that there is none like him on the earth."* It is quite the compliment when God says you are the best on the whole earth. However, Satan asks permission to torment Job. God gives permission. Job loses his property and even his children. He ends up in the dust suffering from boils on him. After several of chapters of "friends" belittling him, he gives his final appeal. Within this defense, 31:6 is unique in that it is one of the only verses in the Bible that is entirely in parenthesis, *"(Let me be weighed in a just balance, and let God know my integrity!)"* Job refers to balance. He wants to make sure both sides are equal.

Balance is necessary for everyone. It is of particular importance for the addict. One wrong move and they lose their balance. They fall. They lose. They need to have a balance between doing and being.

1. On the outside, you need to do things differently. Your actions say a lot. Sometimes people cannot hear what you are saying because your actions are speaking so loud. You need to do things differently to keep balance and stay clean. You cannot do the things you were doing and expect to stay clean. You might have to change your routine. You might need to avoid the old neighborhood. Things need to change. If you keep going back to the old routine, you will use again. You will look and even act like a dog chasing his tail. You will be all out of balance.

2. On the inside, you need to be different. If there is no change on the inside, there will be no lasting change on the outside. No matter how hard you try, only God can change you on the inside. Remember: You can't do it, but it can be done. God can change

you. He can make you better and complete. He can give you joy, peace, and patience. Without proper balance, you will fall.

Job understood this concept. Le uts look at Job 1:1 again, *"There was a man in the land of Uz whose name was Job, and that man was blameless and upright, one who feared God and turned away from evil."*

He was *"blameless and upright."* He knew how to do things differently, correctly. He lived a righteous life.

Then the passage reminds us of how he did it; he feared God. This was the inside. He *"feared God."* That included awe, respect, and love.

Finally, the verse says he *"turned away from evil."* His inward conviction again affected his outward action. He had a right balance between doing and being.

'Blondin' understood balance. I imagine of all the people there; most felt he could not do it and some were hoping he would fall. Life can be like the wind and knock you off balance. God's peace is the only way to change you on the inside. Good balance is not easy; neither is overcoming addiction. Each step is important. One wrong step can have devastating results.

You have to do things differently and be different. Let God change your mind, heart, and soul. Then you can do things differently. God desires to live within you and walk with you.

Be different, changed, transformed, committed, joyful, and balanced.

Is your life balanced?

_____

_____

_____

What changes need to be made?

_____

_____

_____

_____

_____

28

WHAT IS IMPORTANT?

T he international space station toilet costs $19 million. Seriously, I know it can be important to find a bathroom no matter where you are, but $19 million? I guess in a world (or beyond the world) of supply and demand this makes sense, but there is a gold toilet on earth (in Hong Kong) valued at $5 million. When people spend that kind of money, or can I say waste that kind of money, it makes one wonder what is important to them.

This book is written because you are important. God loves people. He loves addicts, inmates, and even people who buy expensive toilets. You are important to God; you are important to us.

I thought I heard it all when I found out about a gold toilet, but then I discovered there is toilet paper in Dubai made with 22-carat gold flakes in it. A roll costs $1,376,900.00 dollars. Seriously?

What is really valuable – people, you!

Matthew 9:9 sounds like a very simple interaction, *"As Jesus passed on from there, he saw a man called Matthew sitting at the tax booth, and he said to him, 'Follow me.' And he rose and followed him."* However, there is a lot going on here that is only known by understanding their culture. Matthew was a tax collector. The Jews did not like tax collectors. The Jews hated tax collectors. They hated Matthew. A tax collector sold himself out to money, greed, and the Romans. Matthew was a Jew who turned on his people to represent Rome. He would then insist on the Jews (even family and friends) to pay him their taxes (by the way, it was common practice to raise the cost and pocket the extra). If they did not pay, he had them thrown in prison or worse.

Next, we have Jesus at Matthew's house, *"And as Jesus reclined at table in the house, behold, many tax collectors and sinners came and were reclining with Jesus and his disciples. And when the Pharisees saw this, they said to his disciples, 'Why does your teacher eat with tax collectors and sinners?' But when he heard it, he said, 'Those who are well have no need of a physician, but those who are sick'"* (Matthew 9:10-12). Jesus went to Matthew's house. This would have been crazy. The "religious" ones were confused; however, it is clear. ALL people are important to Jesus. Yes, even sinners. Yes, even addicts. Yes, even inmates.

The church was not designed for just "good" people; it is just as much for sinners.

You are so important to God that He sent His only Son to die for your sins so you could be forgiven and have the opportunity to accept eternal life. Knowing this, you should respond with three steps.

1. **Talk.** The first step is prayer. Prayer can sound very intimidating, but it is just talking with God. Talk with God; ask Jesus to come into your life. He will!

2. **Turn.** When you ask Jesus into your life, it should make you want to turn from sin. This is called repentance. It means to make a 180-degree turn. It starts with confession, *"If we confess our sins, he is faithful and just to forgive us our sins and to cleanse us from all unrighteousness"* (1 John 1:9). You tell God you understand your sin and the mess it has and could cause. You tell God you have a problem. He wants to hear from you. Repentance is a complete reversal from your sin and old bad habits. You go from focusing on yourself to looking to Jesus for direction. It is not thinking less of yourself; it is thinking of yourself less. Saying you are sorry is not enough.

3. **Transform.** You need to change; it is time for a total transformation. You need to change who you hang out with, where you go, and what you do. Romans 12:2 says, *"Do not be conformed to this world, but be transformed by the renewal of your mind, that by testing you may discern what is the will of God, what is good and acceptable and perfect."* You need to stop being like the world, step up, and be transformed. By thinking and acting correctly, you will learn to find out what pleases God. You will find God's will for your life. You will find a better life.

This will take a lot of dedication. It is not easy. There is no such thing as kind of dedicated. It is all or nothing. You are either all in or not in at all.

Guys often show their love to their gal with gifts of flowers, chocolates, and maybe even jewelry. However, Shahrukh Khan is known for giving loved ones a car. Edward McLean took it to another degree when he bought his sweetheart a $12 million necklace. Not to be outdone, Anil Ambani gave his wife an $84 million yacht. I am not sure these items are worth their price tag.

What is really valuable – people, you!

You are so valuable that Jesus gave Himself for you. He died so you could live. He is not asking you to die for Him. He wants you to have life. It is to be a life full of meaning, purpose, and hope.

Do you realize you are valuable to God?

_____

_____

_____

Write out a prayer thanking God.

_____

_____

_____

_____

_____

_____

_____

_____

_____

_____

29

REESE'S

T here are some things that go great together: Bread and butter, fish and chips, cheese and macaroni, peaches and cream, milk and cookies, and of course peanut butter and chocolate.

Reese's Peanut Butter Cups were first created about ninety years ago. In 1895, John Kellogg (the same guy who created Kellogg cereals) patented a process for making peanut butter. Thirty-three years later, H.B. Reese, while working for Milton Hershey (yes, the Hershey chocolate guy), put peanut butter in chocolate cups. They make a great combination. We sure do not want to see them go to waste (or should I say waist).

It is great when two things come together in such a way that they are better together than they would be on their own. Sometimes one plus one is more than two.

Philip was one of the great guys in the Bible, but we do not know a lot about him. In Acts 8:29-30 God tells him to speak to an Ethiopian official, ***"And the Spirit said to Philip, 'Go over and join this chariot.' So Philip ran to him and heard him reading Isaiah the prophet and asked, 'Do you understand*** *what you are reading?"* The official is reading from the Old Testament but does not understand it. He wants the truth. He has traveled some 1,600 miles. He is searching. He asks Philip some questions. When someone is trying to figure it out, it is good to come along side and help.

Verses 35-38 tell us what happened next, *"Then Philip opened his mouth, and beginning with this Scripture he told him the good news about Jesus. And as they were going along the road they came to some water, and the eunuch said, 'See, here is water! What prevents me from being baptized?' And he commanded the chariot to stop, and they both went down into the water, Philip and the eunuch, and he baptized him."* Philip told the man about Jesus, and the man asked Jesus into his life. When the man saw some water, he requested to be baptized. He made an inward decision which he knew must be followed with an outward action. The two must go together.

An addict will always be an addict. It appears 95% will fall again. The main reason for all of the struggle is that addicts are told to start from the outside. You are told to do certain things instead of being a different person, thinking a different way. Start with your heart. Jesus is the only way to clean up, but it is from the inside out. It cannot happen from the outside in. It must happen from the inside first. Give your life to Christ and start living for Him. The Ethiopian official was trying to figure it out. When it made sense, Philip baptized him as an outward declaration of what had already happened on the inside. You cannot deal with the outside until you have had God deal with the inside. Once you are changed on the inside, you will see that your habits need to change. You will find that the places and people you use to associate with will not help you.

It is good seeing when two things go well together. The Guinness Book of World Records lists the longest marriage as 86 years, 290 days by Herbert and Zelmyra Fisher from North Carolina. However, BBC News reported that Karam and Kartari Chand of England were married for 90 years, 291 days. They said the key is to, "Never argue."

Two other things that have to go together are the outside with the inside. They are kind of married and cannot be separated. As a follower of Jesus, our outward actions have to match our inward belief. When we ask Jesus into our life, our thinking and doing must change.

Do your actions match your heart?

_____

_____

_____

Which needs improving?

_____

_____

_____

_____

_____

30

DEM BONES

D id you know you were born with 270 bones? Several of them fuse together, so adults only have 206 bones. Whenever I think of bones, my mind starts singing that song, "Dem Bones."

Toe bone connected to the foot bone
Foot bone connected to the heel bone
Heel bone connected to the ankle bone
Ankle bone connected to the shin bone
Shin bone connected to the knee bone
Knee bone connected to the thigh bone
Thigh bone connected to the hip bone
Hip bone connected to the back bone
Back bone connected to the shoulder bone
Shoulder bone connected to the neck bone
Neck bone connected to the head bone
Now hear the word of the Lord.

Dem bones, dem bones gonna walk around.
Dem bones, dem bones gonna walk around.
Dem bones, dem bones gonna walk around.
Now hear the word of the Lord.

Although the song is so famous, it actually starts:
Ezekiel connected dem dry bones,
Ezekiel connected dem dry bones,
Ezekiel in the Valley of Dry Bones,
Now hear the word of the Lord.

The Ezekiel this song talks about was a prophet in the Bible. He describes the situation in Ezekiel 37:1-3, *"The hand of the Lord was upon me, and he brought me out in the Spirit of the Lord and set me down in the middle of the valley; it was full of bones. And he led me around among them, and behold, there were very many on the surface of the valley, and behold, they were very dry. And he said to me, 'Son of man, can these bones live?' And I answered, 'O Lord God, you know.'"* Ezekiel ends up in the middle of a valley full of bones. They are all dead and dried up. God asked Ezekiel if he thought He could bring these bones back to life. Ezekiel said he knew God could do it. God can do anything. God did do it. He strengthened the bones. He put flesh, muscle, and tissue on the bones. He even breathed life into those dead bodies. They came alive. They became an army.

God created Heaven and Earth out of nothing. They were created out of thin air. There was nothing, and God made something. If God can create something out of nothing, giving life to something that already exists is easy for Him. Ezekiel knew God could bring the bones back to life and He did.

The addiction world is life the valley of dry bones. It is a valley of death. Addiction may not kill you physically yet, but it will kill all other areas of your life: your family, relationships, money, trust, dreams...etc. God wants the "dry bones" of your life to come alive.

The Lord told Ezekiel to speak to the bones. God will send people into your life to speak truth and life. It gives you the opportunity to be alive in Christ. Hear the Word of the Lord. The addiction world only speaks death into your life. Only God can breathe life into your life and strengthen your bones and flesh. Let God speak into your life.

Addicts cannot protect themselves. Only God can breathe life into your life. Things never turn out the way you expect as an addict. God wants to give you life. He wants a relationship with you. He wants to talk to a living soul, not a pile of dry bones.

Evel Knievel was known for showing off by doing dangerous motorcycle exhibitions. He would attempt to jump his motorcycle over sixteen cars all lined up, a shark tank, the fountains at Caesar's Palace, and even the Snake River Canyon. He often wiped out. He is listed in the Guinness Book of World Records for most bones broken in a lifetime. He broke 433 bones. Although he would nearly break every bone in his body, he continued to get up and try again. His bones would heal, and he would plan another stunt.

Bones do heal. Ezekiel got to see bones not only recover but regain life. Do not give up. Your addiction does not have to kill you. God has a better plan.

Are you ready to let God take control of your life?

_____

What areas of your life do you need to give to Him?

_____
_____
_____

31

DO YOU LOVE ME?

E very year someone takes his girl to the ballpark and then sometime around the seventh inning stretch, with the big screen focusing on him, he drops to a knee and pulls out an engagement ring. He then says those famous words, "Will you marry me?" Hopefully, he does not strike out.

In 2004 Molly Fitzpatrick researched how much it cost for a stadium to put the proposal on the big screen. Five stadiums do not even do it. Prices ranged for the other stadiums. The best deal was the Pirates at $39, while the Reds ($50), Tigers ($75), and Yankees ($100) were not far off. The Indians seemed expensive ($400) until you found out what the Nationals ($1500) and Dodgers ($2500) charge.

Is a ballgame the place the girl wants to attend? Is the guy picking the best place to show his love?

Jesus lets us know how He wants us to express out love to Him. John 14:15 says, *"If you love me, you will keep my commandments."* As we all have experienced, words are nice but not enough. Talk is cheap. Real love includes actions. Jesus says He wants to see that we love Him. Our life needs to show Him that He is #1 in our life.

In John 21:15 Jesus asks 'the question' to Simon Peter, *"When they had finished breakfast, Jesus said to Simon Peter, 'Simon, son of John, do you love me more than these?' He said to him, 'Yes, Lord; you know that I love you.' He said to him, 'Feed my lambs.'"* Peter had just caught 153 fish at one time. It was his record catch. It was his best fishing day ever. He was a fisherman, and he had some stories to tell. After this catch, Jesus asks him, "Do you love me more than all of this?" Even though Peter was experiencing the fisherman high, he says, "Yes." Jesus asks three times, and Peter responds the same way all three times. Jesus tells him to live like it.

Why did Jesus ask Peter three times if he loved Him? Luke 22:56-60 gives the answer, *"And a servant-girl, seeing him as he sat in the firelight and looking intently at him, said, 'This man was with Him too.' But he denied it, saying, 'Woman, I do not know Him.' A little later, another saw him and said, 'You are one of them too!' But Peter said, 'Man, I am not!' After about an hour had passed, another man began to insist, saying, 'Certainly this man also was with Him, for he is a Galilean too.' But Peter said, 'Man, I do not know what you are talking about.' Immediately, while he was still speaking, a rooster crowed."* Peter denied Jesus three times. Jesus asked Peter if he loved Him three times. It was Jesus' way of restoring Peter. Jesus will restore us every time we fail Him. It shows he is forgiven. It shows he was reinstated as a follower of Jesus and leader among the men.

In Matthew 22:36 Jesus is asked, *"Teacher, which is the great commandment in the Law?"* Jesus says it is to love God with everything you have. It is finally expressed in how we treat others. We are to obey God, and this extends to how we treat each other. We tell God we love Him by showing it.

Psalm 139:23-24 contains a prayer that we should say every night, *"Search me, O God, and know my heart! Try me and know my thoughts! And see if there be any grievous way in me, and lead me in the way everlasting!"* Our love for God should lead us to ask Him if there is anything we do that hurts Him. I do not want to hurt my wife, so I am careful about what I do and say. I try to figure out what she likes me to do for her. I need to do this with God. I need to strive to do things that please Him. I need to show my love.

When I was younger, I remember watching Rollen Stewart at major sporting events. I did not know his name, but we just called him Rainbow Man. He would wear a rainbow-colored afro-style wig while holding up a sign that read, "John 3:16." I believe it was his way of telling others about Jesus and telling Jesus he loved Him. A lot of people thought he was crazy, but just about everyone respected his attempt. Love can make us do crazy things.

What are some things you do that prove your love for Christ?

_____
_____
_____
_____
_____

32

DIS-ABLE-R

Dion Rich is the ultimate con man. He has been called the Godfather of the Gatecrash and the Sultan of the Sneak-In. According to the Rolling Stone, he snuck into nineteen straight Super Bowls, gets on the field, and is often in the pictures of the trophy presentation. He does not buy a ticket. He has slipped through a side door, sneak on a team bus, pretend he was an assistant coach, and even dress like an NFL referee. The NFL now hires eight private investigators to follow him so he cannot do it again.

On one occasion, Dion had a friend push him right by the guards in a wheelchair. Was that friend a helper or an enabler? Is he an accessory to the crime? It might sound funny for the Super Bowl, but enablers are not being funny in the addiction world.

It is amazing how the Bible relates to all areas of our life. Genesis 27:6 sounds pretty innocent, *"Rebekah said to her son Jacob, 'I heard your father speak to your brother Esau.'"* Jacob and Esau were twin brothers. Esau was born first, so he was in line for the family blessing and a double portion of the inheritance. He would get to make all the calls and get twice as much of the inheritance. Jacob had already kind of manipulated or took advantage of Esau at a vulnerable time to get his birthright. Now, Jacob wanted his blessing. It was wrong for him to do this. His mother enabled him. She was an enabler. The Bible shows us an enabler.

"Rebekah said to her son Jacob, 'I heard your father speak to your brother Esau.'" Isaac told Esau to prepare a meal for him. It was time for the family blessing to be given to him. Isaac was blind. Rebekah loved her son Jacob more than her son Esau. She makes a plan to help Jacob still the blessing. She was an enabler. She was an accomplice. She was an accessory to the crime. She was a partner in crime.

Jacob cons his dad and steals the blessing. When Esau finds out, he is furious. He wants to kill his brother. Jacob has to run for his life. He moves away. He does not see his parents or brother for 20 years. Mom helped split the family.

Sometimes we miss how harmful an enabler is. They are not enabling anyone to do good. I think they should be called a dis-able-r. They are making it so their friend or a family member are 'not able' to accomplish goals or succeed in life.

There are four key points in not being consumed by the enabler's words and world.

1. Realize the difference between an enabler and a helper. An enabler will give an addict money; a helper will give him food. Warn your family of the difference.

2. Learn to recognize the enablers around you. Identify who is a helper and who is an enabler. The enemy will use enablers to destroy an addict. Be responsible. Warn your enabler.

3. Learn how to resist the enabler. Stop blaming the enabler for your relapse. Addicts need help, but not a yes man. Do not enable the enabler. Put a plan in place to eliminate the voice of the enabler from reaching you. Block your phone. Avoid them.

4. Rely on someone who will shoot straight with you. Find someone who will help you with your plan to stay clean. Allow this person to point out who the enablers are in your life. Be honest with yourself. Do not hit bottom. Get a hold of your scheming. Be honest with yourself so you can let someone else be honest with you.

You need a helper, not an enabler. An enabler seems kind, loving, and helpful, but they are selfish and destructive. Real friends empower you. They are willing to tell you the truth even when it hurts. They do not like making you mad at them, but they are willing to take one for the team. Remember, it takes a team all going in the same direction with the same goals to win.

What is your plan to stop the enemy from destroying you?

_____

_____

_____

_____

_____

33

HIDE-N-SEEK

D id the ever play Hide-n-Seek as a kid? According to Guinness World Records, two companies initiated the largest game of Hide-n-Seek ever involving 1,437 people in Chengdu, Sichuan, China. It occurred on January 1, 2014. I am not sure New Year's Day is a day many people want to be found.

It can be fun and funny playing Hide-n-Seek with a child. So often they believe that if they cannot see you, then you cannot see them. It might be as simple as them covering their eyes with their hands to hiding behind curtains with their legs hanging out. They are easy to find. It sounds silly until we realize that a lot of adults try playing Hide-n-Seek from God.

David writes Psalm 139. The chapter challenges us in that we can never hide from God, but it is designed to encourage us that we are never out of sight from God. He has everything in control. He is watching.

The first six verses remind us that God knows everything, *"O LORD, You have searched me and known me. You know when I sit down and when I rise up; You understand my thought from afar. You scrutinize my path and my lying down, And are intimately acquainted with all my ways. Even before there is a word on my tongue, Behold, O LORD, You know it all. You have enclosed me behind and before, And laid Your hand upon me. Such knowledge is too wonderful for me; It is too high, I cannot attain to it."* He knows the past, present, and even future. God knows us better than we know ourselves. He knows our thoughts, words, and actions before they even happen. God has searched us and knows who we are.

Verses seven through twelve remind us that God is everywhere. *"Where can I go from Your Spirit? Or where can I flee from Your presence? If I ascend to heaven, You are there; If I make my bed in Sheol, behold, You are there. If I take the wings of the dawn, If I dwell in the remotest part of the sea, Even there Your hand will lead me, And Your right hand will lay hold of me. If I say, 'Surely the darkness will overwhelm me, And the light around me will be night,' Even the darkness is not dark to You, And the night is as bright as the day. Darkness and light are alike to You."* You cannot run from God. He knows every intimate detail of your life. You cannot hide from God. As we are aware, Jonah figured this out. Not even darkness stops God from seeing everything about you.

Verses thirteen through eighteen remind us that God is all-powerful.

"For You formed my inward parts; You wove me in my mother's womb. I will give thanks to You, for I am fearfully and wonderfully made; Wonderful are Your works, And my soul knows it very well. My frame was not hidden from You, When I was made in secret, And skillfully wrought in the depths of the earth; Your eyes have seen my unformed

140

substance; And in Your book were all written The days that were ordained for me, When as yet there was not one of them. How precious also are Your thoughts to me, O God! How vast is the sum of them! If I should count them, they would outnumber the sand. When I awake, I am still with You." God knows our every thought, word, and action. He always sees us. We cannot hide from Him. With this all said, these verses let us know He is crazy about us. God is crazy about you. He loves you regardless of your past. His love is pure and matchless, anything else is not God. God still has dreams and plans for you. You cannot out dream God. Dream big; God can handle it. God's dream for you is greater than you can imagine (more than the number of grains of sand). The enemy wants you to give up on your dreams. People will try to rob you of your dreams. Life will try to rob you of your dreams. Haters will hate. People will get jealous. Press forward.

Proverbs 15:3 adds, *"The eyes of the LORD are in every place, keeping watch on the evil and the good."* Too many people think God watches us so that He can catch us doing something wrong and zap us. That is so harsh and unloving. Although He is a God of justice, realize He is watching the good. He wants to bless you.

You cannot hide from God. He knows your actions, words, thoughts, and dreams. Give them all to Him. Live for Him and get ready to be blessed.

What are your goals and dreams?

_____

_____

_____

_____

_____

_____

What are you praying for?

_____

_____

_____

_____

_____

_____

_____

_____

34

MEDIATOR

D on Meyer was the winningest coach for men's college basketball until recently when Duke University coach Mike Krzyzewski (Coach K) surpassed him. Meyer had 923 wins (only 324 losses). He received numerous awards, yet said, "Anytime you get an award as a coach, you've got to be the ultimate fool to think it wasn't your assistant coaches and all the players responsible for the award."

Everyone knows you have to have the players, but assistant coaches can be so valuable. I found it interesting that the Detroit Lions and Cleveland Browns each have 21 assistant coaches (oddly enough the Super Bowl Champion New England Patriots only list 14). The assistant coach is a mediator or go-between for the player and the head coach. The head coach is looking at the big picture while each assistant coach works individually with his unit. Sometimes it may feel like all the head coach does is well, while the assistant is there for encouragement and personal direction.

Everyone needs a mediator, a go-between, or someone who helps take a stand for us. This is particularly the case for the addict. The Bible records a story about a beautiful woman who was that mediator for her wicked husband.

In 1 Samuel 25:8-9 we read, *"Ask your young men, and they will tell you. Therefore let my young men find favor in your eyes, for we come on a feast day. Please give whatever you have at hand to your servants and to your son David. When David's young men came, they said all this to Nabal in the name of David, and then they waited."* David was not king yet. He was on the run from Saul. So, to make ends meet, he provided security for farmers and shepherds. He had a following of men who protected people. In exchange, they would feed these guys. It was an actual "work for food" scenario. The men have worked, and they go to this rich man named Nabal and ask for payment. Nabal brushed them off. He refused. When David found out, he told the men to get their swords. It was game time.

Verses 14-17 continue the story, *"But one of the young men told Abigail, Nabal's wife, 'Behold, David sent messengers out of the wilderness to greet our master, and he railed at them. Yet the men were very good to us, and we suffered no harm, and we did not miss anything when we were in the fields, as long as we went with them. They were a wall to us both by night and by day, all the while we were with them keeping the sheep. Now therefore know this and consider what you should do, for harm is determined against our master and against all his house, and he is such a worthless man that one cannot speak to him.'"* One of Nabal's servants witnessed the confrontation and told Abigail. He knew Nabal would not listen so he kind of went to the assistant coach, Nabal's wife. She took action. Verse 18 starts with a menu, *"Then Abigail made haste and took two hundred loaves and two skins of wine and five sheep already prepared and five seahs of parched grain and a hundred clusters of raisins and two hundred cakes of figs, and laid them on donkeys."* Abigail goes as a mediator between David and Nabal. She works on behalf of her husband. She begs for mercy saying, *"Please forgive the trespass of your servant. For the LORD will certainly make my lord a sure house, because my lord is fighting the battles of the LORD, and evil shall not be found in you so long as you live"* (verse 28). David accepts her peace offering. Verses 34-35 say, *"'For as surely as the LORD, the God of Israel, lives, who has restrained me from hurting you, unless you had hurried and come to meet me, truly by morning there had not been left to Nabal so much as one male.' Then David received from her hand what she had brought him. And he said to her, 'Go up in peace to your house. See, I have obeyed your voice, and I have granted your petition.'"* David was ready to kill every man. Abigail stepped in-between and saved their lives.

Nabal was a bad guy. He was a wicked man. His name even means fool or senseless. He was a mess. He did wrong things and made poor decisions. Fortunately, Nabal had a wise wife, Abigail.

We are all like Nabal. We have made a mess of our lives and disaster is coming. God is just and requires justice. Our sin brings a payment. Payment we cannot even afford. Fortunately, 1 Timothy 2:5 says, *"For there is one God, and there is one mediator between God and men, the man Christ Jesus."* Jesus stepped in and paid the payment for our sin. He went in on our behalf. He was our mediator. It will save your life if you are willing to accept Him.

What made Nabal a mess? The Bible tells us he was a user, probably alcohol. His addiction ended up costing him his life and his wife. Addiction will cost you. If you think it will not, you have bought the lie of the enemy. It appears Nabal drank himself to death. Addiction will end up killing you. It is not a matter of 'if but a question of 'when.' Addiction is a thief; it will always take more than you want to give. It takes more time that you expect. It takes more money than you want to pay. It will cost you. There is hope: Jesus stepped in-between us and the wrath of God.

Abraham Lincoln was a lawyer before becoming president. He is credited with a humorous quote, "He who represents himself has a fool for a client." He was reminding everyone that we need help, especially in the court of law. It is true in daily life, too.

Who can you trust? Who has your back and will help you beat this addiction?

_____

_____

_____

Who are you helping?

_____

_____

_____

35

ANCHORMAN

The Darwin Awards records a story about something called 'shopping cart game.' The game is played by tying a rope to a shopping cart, the other end to an anchor, someone getting in the cart, and then riding the cart off a dock into a lake. They then use the rope to pull the cart back to shore. One late night/early morning after too much drinking, Chance thought it would be a good idea to be the 'anchor' for someone and tie the cart to his belt. As you can imagine, once the cart hit the water it pulled Chance in with the cart and rider. The cart sunk to the bottom holding Chance underwater too long. His family is sharing his story reminding people to think before they act.

Choices have consequences. Think about what you are thinking about. A wrong decision can cost you your life. The Bible records a story involving Paul, Barnabas, and Mark. It did not cost anyone their life, but one man's decision cost him and affected others.

Paul and Barnabas were the world's first missionaries. They were heroes of the faith. In Acts 15 they decide to visit some of the places they have preached at to see how they are doing. Verse 36 says, *"After some days Paul said to Barnabas, 'Let us return and visit the brethren in every city in which we proclaimed the word of the Lord, and see how they are.'"* They decided to go. Verses 37-39 take us into some of the behind the scenes confrontation, *"Barnabas wanted to take John, called Mark, along with them also. But Paul kept insisting that they should not take him along who had deserted them in Pamphylia and had not gone with them to the work. And there occurred such a sharp disagreement that they separated from one another, and Barnabas took Mark with him and sailed away to Cyprus."* Barnabas wants to take John Mark with them, but Paul does not trust Mark. It appears Mark bailed on them before and Paul does not want to risk it again. This caused a *"sharp disagreement."* They split up and went their separate ways. Barnabas took Mark with him, Paul took Silas, and they went in different directions.

There is quite the debate on who was right, Paul or Barnabas? Scripture does not tell us. It is not important, but there are four things that you need to understand from this story.

1. Choices have consequences. Good choices have helped you, but bad choices are haunting you. Paul says that Mark's relapse in Pamphylia has consequences. He would not, could not, or at least did not trust him anymore. Mark missed out on an opportunity to touch many lives in a positive way. Because of a bad choice, a price had to be paid.

2. Your decisions affect others. The Bible says that your choices will affect your children, grandchildren, and even great-grandchildren. It has been said that no man is an island. Your choices have affected other family members, friends, and even people you do not know. Mark's decision changed Paul and Barnabas. Sometimes your choices will cause other to split up. It may cause others to choose 'sides.'

3. You need to set boundaries. Mark should have set his mission like Joshua did to choose whom he would serve. Joshua said he would serve the Lord. He then decided to have tunnel vision, to set boundaries, and to live between the lines. Paul also set limits. He did not want missionaries around him who were not focused. He was very particular who he wanted on his team. He had to much work to do to get sidetracked. Get off the fence. You need to live between the lines. If you live between the lines, you will not have to worry about repercussions for bad decisions. You can be the person God intended you to be.

4. You can be restored. There are people who will trust you again. Barnabas was known for encouragement. He gave Mark another chance. He believed in him. Pray that God will bring a trustworthy friend who will trust you and give you another chance, but make sure you set boundaries, so you do not mess up again. Most people live by that old saying, "Fool me once, shame on you; fool me twice, shame on me." They are willing to give you another chance but do not blow it.

You might be wondering whatever happened to Mark. Paul writes 2 Timothy 4:11 late in his life when he is getting ready to die, *"Luke alone is with me. Get Mark and bring him with you, for he is very useful to me for ministry."* Paul realizes that Mark became a changed man. Mark had become an important part of the team. Paul wanted Mark around him. Paul noticed the change and believed in him. Mark was restored.

Darwin Awards records a story about 22-year-old Ryan. It appears he was bored one night, so he decided to grab a rope, hop a construction site security fence, climbs a 10-story crane, ties the rope to the boom, and starts swinging. Unfortunately, he did not look out for overhead wires and swung right into his death. The story has a horrible ending, but it reminds us that our choices have consequences. Sometimes we do not get a chance to be restored.

What bad decisions have you made?

_____

_____

_____

_____

_____

_____

What choices do you need to make now?

_____

_____

_____

_____

_____

_____

_____

_____

_____

_____

_____

36

TRANSFORMER

T he Better Sleep Council mentions a number of interesting things about sleep: about 12% of people only dream in black and white, sleep positions may determine or reveal someone's personality, Koalas sleep about 22 hours a day while giraffes sleep less than 2 hours a day, and that dolphin only shut down half their brain when they sleep because they need the other half to help with breathing cycles. It seems odd to think of a dolphin drowning.

Although these items are interesting about sleep, one of the funniest stories about sleeping is in the Bible. Paul was one of the greatest preachers of all time. He had been speaking all day when we come to Acts 20:9, *"And a young man named Eutychus, sitting at the window, sank into a deep sleep as Paul talked still longer. And being overcome by sleep, he fell down from the third story and was taken up dead."* The guy fell asleep in church and fell out of the balcony. I must admit my initial response is to laugh. It is okay; the passage goes on to say that God heals the man showing His power and validating Paul's ministry. So we can laugh that a man fell asleep in church and fell three stories. Too bad they did not have YouTube back then. We have all seen the guy bob his head as he is struggling to stay awake, but fall out of the balcony?

I imagine he woke up quite embarrassed. People need to wake up today. The world is forming us without us realizing it. We are slipping off. We need to be transformed. Romans 12:2 says, *"Do not be conformed to this world, but be transformed by the renewal of your mind, that by testing you may discern what is the will of God, what is good and acceptable and perfect."* You need to stop letting the world say who you are. Wake up and be transformed. This transformation can be seen in three areas.

1. There has to be an eternal transformation.
Sometimes we struggle with old things. When we become a follower of Jesus, the old has passed away. Romans 6:6 says, *"We know that our old self was crucified with him in order that the body of sin might be brought to nothing, so that we would no longer be enslaved to sin."* The old man is crucified with Christ that the body of sin might be destroyed. You do not need to serve sin or the desires of the old man. The Bible goes on to say you are a new creation in Christ, *"Therefore, if anyone is in Christ, he is a new creation. The old has passed away; behold, the new has come"* (2 Corinthians 5:17). You are a new creation in Christ; you can claim the victory over the old self. You are a new man.

2. There has to be an internal transformation.
You need to have an eternal transformation before you can have an internal transformation. You cannot do it alone. God will help you. He makes a comforting promise in 1 Corinthians 10:13, *"No temptation has overtaken you that is not common to man. God is faithful, and he will not let you be tempted beyond your ability, but with the temptation he will also provide the way of escape, that you may be able to endure it."* The old self will show its ugly head, but God has made it so that you do not have to lose. You can win. He will help you. You will not be tempted beyond what you can stand.

3. There has to be an external transformation.

Just like you have to have an eternal transformation before internal transformation, you have to have the internal transformation before you can genuinely have an external transformation. When you have an eternal and internal transformation, it will be reflected in an external transformation. It is shown in how you act, serve, and obey God's commandments. The right desires only come from you and your good decisions. The change needs to be seen in the fruit in your life. Ephesians 4:22 tells you, *"To put off your old self, which belongs to your former manner of life and is corrupt through deceitful desires."* Vulgar talk and actions of the old man must be removed. There has to be a change in your life and show it in everyday life. Colossians 3:9 adds, *"Do not lie to one another, seeing that you have put off the old self with its practices."* Do not lie to yourself or others. You cannot lie to God. Your life should be the proof of a new life in Christ. Change your desire. Check your language. Check your lying tongue. Check your actions. Integrity is doing the right thing when no one is watching. By the way, God is always watching.

A horrible picture is a story about the frog. If you put a frog in hot water, it will naturally jump out. However, if you put the same frog in room temperature water and slowly raise the heat, it will eventually stay in boiling water and die.

As an addict, you need to wake up. Stop being conformed to the world. Be transformed. Change. Grow. Live. Be a new person.

What areas of your life are holding you back?

_____

_____

_____

_____

_____

How will you change?

_____

_____

_____

_____

_____

_____

_____

37

WON AND OH

Everyone loves a winner. As soon as a team starts winning, a lot of people jump on the bandwagon. For teams to have won, someone else had to lose. It is surprising to see some of the longest losing streaks in sport's history:

MLB - Philadelphia Phillies lost 23 straight (1961).
NHL - Winnipeg Jets had 25 straight winless games (1980).
NFL - Tampa Bay Buccaneers lost 26 straight (1976–77).
NBA - Philadelphia 76ers lost 28 straight games (2014–16).

However, the craziest losing streak of all time was the Prairie View Panthers. Although they won five championships in the 50's and 60's, they lost 80 straight games in the 90's.

Even though losing streaks catch the news, addicts cannot afford to lose. There is too much at stake. You have to win. Losing is not an option. 1 Samuel 17 records one of the most famous Bible stories – David and Goliath. We love the story because an average guy like us takes on his giant and wins.

1. Start small and build up to the big giants in your life. Verses 34-36 say, ***"But David said to Saul, 'Your servant used to***

keep sheep for his father. And when there came a lion, or a bear, and took a lamb from the flock, I went after him and struck him and delivered it out of his mouth. And if he arose against me, I caught him by his beard and struck him and killed him. Your servant has struck down both lions and bears, and this uncircumcised Philistine shall be like one of them, for he has defied the armies of the living God.'" David started off as a shepherd. He killed a lion and a bear. He handled smaller giants and was now ready for a bigger monster. Get victory over the little things before you gain victory over the enormous things in life. Start small. Start hanging out with the right people to fend off the big things in your life. Start small and build up to the big giants in your life.

2. You have to overcome the negative statements people say to you. You can win. David did not get full support from his brothers. Verse 28 says, *"Now Eliab his eldest brother heard when he spoke to the men. And Eliab's anger was kindled against David, and he said, 'Why have you come down? And with whom have you left those few sheep in the wilderness? I know your presumption and the evil of your heart, for you have come down to see the battle.'"* David tried to do the right thing, and even his family shot him down. He was criticized. They did not believe him, support him, or even encourage him. He did not let others hold him back. You have to believe what God can do in and through you.

3. Be internally motivated daily, even hourly. Honor God. David takes charge in verse 32, *"And David said to Saul, 'Let no man's heart fail because of him. Your servant will go and fight with this Philistine.'"* Verse 37 adds, *"And David said, 'The LORD who delivered me from the paw of the lion and from the paw of the bear will deliver me from the hand of*

this Philistine.' And Saul said to David, 'Go, and the LORD be with you!'" David gives God credit before the battle even starts. David knew what God wanted him to do and he went out and did it. Using dishonors God. Let people know, "Do not get in my way, I have a cause."

4. Be what God made you to be. Saul immediately tries to do what he thinks is best for David, *"Then Saul clothed David with his armor. He put a helmet of bronze on his head and clothed him with a coat of mail, 39and David strapped his sword over his armor. And he tried in vain to go, for he had not tested them. Then David said to Saul, 'I cannot go with these, for I have not tested them.' So David put them off"* (verse 38). Saul meant well, but he tried to change David. Do not let the crowd dictate to you who you should be. Let God dictate to you who you are. Who cares what people think of you? What matters is what God thinks about you! Start acting like God expects you to be.

5. Speak out against the giants in your life. David takes a stand in verses 45-47, *"Then David said to the Philistine, 'You come to me with a sword and with a spear and with a javelin, but I come to you in the name of the LORD of hosts, the God of the armies of Israel, whom you have defied. This day the LORD will deliver you into my hand, and I will strike you down and cut off your head. And I will give the dead bodies of the host of the Philistines this day to the birds of the air and to the wild beasts of the earth, that all the earth may know that there is a God in Israel, and that all this assembly may know that the LORD saves not with sword and spear. For the battle is the LORD's, and he will give you into our hand.'"* David speaks with confidence. He takes a stand. He speaks against the enemy, his giant. You need to identify your enemy and speak against it.

157

6. You can win with God. Verses 49-51 record David's victory, *"And David put his hand in his bag and took out a stone and slung it and struck the Philistine on his forehead. The stone sank into his forehead, and he fell on his face to the ground. So David prevailed over the Philistine with a sling and with a stone, and struck the Philistine and killed him. There was no sword in the hand of David. Then David ran and stood over the Philistine and took his sword and drew it out of its sheath and killed him and cut off his head with it. When the Philistines saw that their champion was dead, they fled."* David killed his giant. He even cut off his head. You too can win.

Maybe you are in the midst of a losing streak. Losing streaks can end. The Prairie View Panthers finally won a game after losing 80 straight. They could be viewed as 1-80 or 1-0. They now had a one-game winning streak. The key is to start small, overcome comments of haters, be internally motivated, be who you were meant to be, speak out against the giants in your life, and win with God. Remember, you can't do it, but it can be done. It can only be done with God!

What is the giant in your life?

_____

_____

_____

What is your next step?

_____

_____

_____

_____

_____

38

MIND-SET

*A*merica's *Toughest Jobs* filmed nine of the craziest actual jobs people have: crab fishing, trucking in Alaska, gold digging, monster trucks, oil drilling, bullfighting, bridge crew, logging, and mountain rescue. Others I have heard that seem over-the-top are the bomb squad, skyscraper window-washing, bounty hunters, miner jobs, and obviously military, police, and firemen. Then I heard of the domestic engineer. The position requires 168 hours of work and being on call. Oh, and there is no paycheck. It is the stay-at-home mom.

Jobs can be tough. That is probably why they call it work.

The Book of Nehemiah is about a man who had a very cushy job. His life was comfortable. However, he saw a problem. The walls of his hometown were broken and needed to be rebuilt. It did not affect him, but Nehemiah stepped out to lead others in fixing the problem. As an addict, you need to work, or you will probably relapse. In chapter four Nehemiah shares four points that help us when we choose to make a difference.

1. Haters will hate. Verse 1-3 describe how outsiders badmouthed them and tried to distract them, *"Now when Sanballat*

heard that we were building the wall, he was angry and greatly enraged, and he jeered at the Jews. And he said in the presence of his brothers and of the army of Samaria, 'What are these feeble Jews doing? Will they restore it for themselves? Will they sacrifice? Will they finish up in a day? Will they revive the stones out of the heaps of rubbish, and burned ones at that?' Tobiah the Ammonite was beside him, and he said, 'Yes, what they are building—if a fox goes up on it he will break down their stone wall!'" When you choose to get clean, you would think everyone would be happy for you, but it is not necessarily the case. People will criticize and bring up the past. You need to be ready. It is wrong. It is sad, but it will happen. Press forward. Get to work.

2. Haters are actually fighting God. In verses 4-5 he clarifies who their battle is with, *"Hear, O our God, for we are despised. Turn back their taunt on their own heads and give them up to be plundered in a land where they are captives. Do not cover their guilt, and let not their sin be blotted out from your sight, for they have provoked you to anger in the presence of the builders."* These haters have provoked God to anger. Hater will hate, but do not take it personally. Realize they are the one with a problem. Let God take care of it. Focus on the work you need to do.

3. You need to put your mind to work. Verse 6 says it plainly, *"So we built the wall. And all the wall was joined together to half its height, for the people had a mind to work."* Amazing things can happen when people put their mind to it. You need the mentality to work and to succeed. Set your mind to it. You have to get to work and being an addict you never get a 'day off' to do whatever you want. You need to work at being clean. The time to get to work is now. Build on your success. Get to work on making

your life. Get rid of the rubbish and trash in your life. You cannot hang out with garbage and not smell of it. Put the trash to the curb, or it will kick you to the curb.

4. Pray! When the trash talking did not stop them, the haters planned on getting physical. They were preparing to fight. Nehemiah gives his response in verse 9, *"And we prayed to our God and set a guard as a protection against them day and night."* Nehemiah prayed. He prayed before the battle even came. Pray! God is the only way to be clean. He is the only One who can help you. You have a God who can make real changes in your life. Ask for His help.

There are all kinds of tough jobs in the world. One of the toughest is rebuilding your life. You need to get focused. Concentrate on building your life. No one can create your life for you. You do not just fix a life; you create it. Plans and lumber do not automatically build a house. It takes workers. The enemy wants to tear your life down and destroy you. Think IMPOSSIBLE. It might look like impossible, but you are saying I M Possible. I can do it through Christ.

Who are the haters in your life?

_____

_____

What work do you need to do to repair your life?

_____

_____

_____

_____

_____

_____

39

PR-I-DE

The Telegraph, National Geographic, and PBS all have substantial information about the infamous Titanic. It was the most impressive ship of its time and the largest movable manmade object in the world measuring 882 feet in length and about 92 feet at its widest point. Movies, museums, and stories of all kinds have been revisited for years.

The Whiter Star Line crew was becoming proud in the massive ships they were producing. Captain Smith earlier had said of one of their ships, "I cannot imagine any condition which would cause a ship to founder. I cannot conceive of any vital disaster happening to this vessel. Modern shipbuilding has gone beyond that." Another employee referenced the Titanic itself in saying, "Not even God himself could sink this ship."

Their arrogance was 'put on ice' on April 15, 1912, when the ship traveled two miles in the wrong direction. It sunk. The first-class passengers had just finished an eleven-course meal when the Titanic hit an iceberg. Confusion was everywhere. They were so sure it could not sink they canceled the lifeboat drill scheduled for the previous days. To make matters worse, they only had enough lifeboats for one-third of the total capacity. Since the call went for women and children first, one guy was noted as dressing like a woman hoping to get on a lifeboat.

A company's pride cost over 1,500 people to die. Pride caused a fall.

This is a common theme in the Bible. James 4:6 says, *"But he gives more grace. Therefore it says, 'God opposes the proud but gives grace to the humble.'"* There is a difference between striving to do well in taking pride in what you do and in being proud. God does not like it when we get proud. God opposes the proud. Pride is a problem. You do not want to be in opposition to God and His beautiful grace. On the flip side, God reaches out to those who are humble.

In John chapter 8 we have a group of guys trying to trap Jesus, *"The scribes and the Pharisees brought a woman who had been caught in adultery, and placing her in the midst they said to him, 'Teacher, this woman has been caught in the act of adultery. Now in the Law, Moses commanded us to stone such women. So what do you say?' This they said to test him, that they might have some charge to bring against him. Jesus bent down and wrote with his finger on the ground"* (verses 3-6). These Scribes and Pharisees were sinister. They had an agenda and did not care who they hurt or affected. Most of the time people do not care about how their actions affect you. They do not have your best interests at heart. Do not be influenced by these people. Be careful with whom you hang out. The rest of the story is primarily based on two points.

1. God opposes the proud. Verses 7-9 give Jesus' response, *"And as they continued to ask him, he stood up and said to them, 'Let him who is without sin among you be the first to throw*

a stone at her.' And once more he bent down and wrote on the ground. But when they heard it, they went away one by one, beginning with the older ones, and Jesus was left alone with the woman standing before him." The obvious problem was this woman, but actually, the deeper problem was the pride of these officials. He gently but directly points it out. We should not judge others. We should not compare ourselves with someone else. We are not that innocent or that good. Matthew 23:12 agrees in saying, *"Whoever exalts himself will be humbled, and whoever humbles himself will be exalted."* Jesus did not view the woman as opposition. It was the pride of these men.

Saint Augustine makes a powerful observation, "It was pride that changed angels into devils; it is humility that makes men as angels." Satan fell because of his pride. He thought he was bigger than God and it cost him forever. Pride causes us to fall. We need humility.

2. God gives grace to the humble. Verses 10-11 give Jesus response to the woman, *"Jesus stood up and said to her, 'Woman, where are they? Has no one condemned you?' She said, 'No one, Lord.' And Jesus said, 'Neither do I condemn you; go, and from now on sin no more.'"* Jesus shows grace. He does not overlook her sin; He tells her to stop living like that. He showed grace. She did not deserve it. We do not deserve it, but Jesus even offers us eternal life, *"For God so loved the world, that he gave his only Son, that whoever believes in him should not perish but have eternal life."*

Proverbs 29:23 adds, *"One's pride will bring him low, but he who is lowly in spirit will obtain honor."* This theme is so common is Scripture. God is repeating Himself, so it must be extra important. 1 Peter 5:5 says, *"Likewise, you who are younger, be subject to the elders. Clothe yourselves, all of you, with humility toward one another, for 'God opposes the proud but gives grace to the humble.'"*

It is not our job to judge or condemn others. Only God has that right, yet He gives us so much grace. John 3:17 adds, *"For God did not send his Son into the world to condemn the world, but in order that the world might be saved through him."* God is so good. He wants to see us get saved.

In what ways are you judging others or struggling with pride?

_____

_____

_____

_____

_____

_____

_____

_____

How will you humble yourself so God can bless you?

_____

_____

_____

_____

_____

_____

_____

_____

40

THE WOW FACTOR

Recently Kyrie Irving, the Cleveland Cavaliers point guard, said, "The Earth is flat. The Earth is flat. The Earth is flat." He even added, "This is not even a conspiracy theory." Seriously, he believes the Earth is flat?

I was taught in Elementary school that Christopher Columbus sailed from Spain in 1492 across the Atlantic Ocean disproving the theory and common belief that the Earth was flat. We have known the Earth is not flat for over 500 years. Research even shows that scientists and philosophers figured this out more than 1,000 years before Columbus sailed.

Since the Earth is a sphere and not flat, there is something called an Earth Curve Calculator. This formula determines how far one can see based on the height of their location. Obviously, you can see further if you climb a tree than you can from the ground.

It is interesting to note that the horizon is about three miles away for a person six-foot tall. He can potentially see three miles. If he wants to see further, he needs to get to a higher point. This sounds pretty basic.

Matthew 14 contains the story of Jesus walking on water. Stop for a minute. Did you catch that? Jesus Walked On Water (WOW)! There are three fundamental truths we need to get from this amazing story.

1. Jesus is watching. Verses 22-24 start the story, *"Immediately he made the disciples get into the boat and go before him to the other side, while he dismissed the crowds. And after he had dismissed the crowds, he went up on the mountain by himself to pray. When evening came, he was there alone, but the boat by this time was a long way from the land, beaten by the waves, for the wind was against them."* The story does not begin on water. It starts on a mountain. Jesus was watching. We all deal with doubt, and there may be seasons of our life when we question God. You ask, "How am I going to get through this?" Whatever storm you are going through, it is not greater than Jesus who lives in you.

Jesus had just fed over 5,000 with just a few fish and bread. He has the disciples get on a boat and sends them across the sea. He tells them that He will catch up with them. He then goes on the mountain to pray. While on top of the mountain, Jesus could see the entire Sea of Galilee. He could see they were headed into a storm. Jesus is always watching.

Psalm 139:7-8 clearly states, *"Where shall I go from your Spirit? Or where shall I flee from your presence? If I ascend to heaven, you are there!"* No matter where we are, no matter what storm we are facing, Jesus is watching.

2. Jesus is willing to help. Verses 25-27 continue the story, *"And in the fourth watch of the night he came to them, walking on the sea. But when the disciples saw him walking on the*

sea, they were terrified, and said, 'It is a ghost!' and they cried out in fear. But immediately Jesus spoke to them, saying, 'Take heart; it is I. Do not be afraid.'" Jesus came down to meet the disciples in the storm. He will always stoop down to come to us during our storms. Jesus is always on His way. He is never late. The disciples were terrified. Jesus showed up in a way they did not expect. Jesus said, *"Take heart; it is I. Do not be afraid."* During storms, we need to be still, quiet, and wait for God. In the middle of a storm listen for God and what He is trying to teach you.

3. Look to Jesus. Verses 28-33 wrap it up saying, *"And Peter answered him, 'Lord, if it is you, command me to come to you on the water.' He said, 'Come.' So Peter got out of the boat and walked on the water and came to Jesus. But when he saw the wind, he was afraid, and beginning to sink he cried out, 'Lord, save me.' Jesus immediately reached out his hand and took hold of him, saying to him, 'O you of little faith, why did you doubt?' And when they got into the boat, the wind ceased. And those in the boat worshiped him, saying, 'Truly you are the Son of God.'"* Peter walks on water. He took some steps on the water. Jesus said, "Come" and he walked on water. The problem came when he started looking at the storm and took his eyes off Jesus. Peter looked at his storm, and he cried out to Jesus. You cannot make it on your own. Ask God and others to help you. Immediately Jesus reached out His hand to save him. Jesus' hand was on Peter; he was protected. Sometimes we get out of touch with Jesus, we sink, and we drown in our circumstances.

We might only be able to see some three miles away on this sphere we call Earth. However, Jesus is not limited. He can always see you. He even knows how to handle that 71% of the Earth that is water. He walks on water. Jesus is watching. He wants to help you. You need to look to Jesus. Hebrews 12:1-2 says, *"Therefore, since we are surrounded by so great a cloud of witnesses, let us also lay aside every weight, and sin which clings so closely, and let us run with endurance the race that is set before us, looking to Jesus, the founder and perfecter of our faith, who for the joy that was set before him endured the cross, despising the shame, and is seated at the right hand of the throne of God."* The key is to look to Jesus.

Is it scary or comforting that Jesus is always watching?

_____

_____

_____

_____

What do you need to do to see Jesus better?

_____

_____

_____

_____

_____

_____

41

OXYMORON

O xymoron sounds like a term one would use to insult another. Is it trash talk? Actually, it describes when you use two words together that are used as opposites when not together. I was _clearly confused_ when I ate some _pretty ugly jumbo shrimp_ at the _goodbye reception_ because it was my _least favorite_ dish and my _only choice_, but it was _awfully good_. It is funny how when we put two words together it can amplify a meaning. It can be _weirdly normal_.

The premise of this book seems the same way: You can't do it, but it can be done. It does not seem to make sense, and it will not make sense in your walk. Only God can make the difference. He changes the IMPOSSIBLE to **I M** POSSIBLE. Yes, it is possible with Him. You can win. Addiction groups do not have the answer. Only Jesus has the answer.

Sometimes life does not even make sense. You can learn from the School of Hard Knocks or the example of others. It is either the hard way or a much less painful way.

1. You can learn the hard way. You can learn from your mistakes. 1 Corinthians 10:12 says, **_"Therefore let anyone who thinks_**

that he stands take heed lest he fall." Pay attention before you fall. Do not go back. If you do not pay attention to what others have done, you will end up learning about handcuffs, court appearances, and the jail cell the hard way. People learn from losing their job, car, house, and family, but there has to be a better way. Are you sick of learning the hard way? Learn from the experience of others. More importantly, learn from the Bible. God's Word has the answer to eternal life and life to the full. John 10:10 says, *"The thief comes only to steal and kill and destroy. I came that they may have life and have it abundantly."* Satan wants to destroy you, but God is offering abundant life. He uses the Bible to direct you. Psalm 119:105 says, *"Your word is a lamp to my feet and a light to my path."* He is willing to direct your next step and your future. You cannot do it alone. You can do it in the power of Christ.

2. You can learn a better way. You can learn from the mistakes of others. Verse 12 warned about walking alone and falling. The verse right before it says, *"Now these things happened to them as an example, but they were written down for our instruction, on whom the end of the ages has come."* Paul says to watch others and learn from their failures and successes. It is so important that Paul had even said it in verse 6, *"Now these things took place as examples for us, that we might not desire evil as they did."* Paul is bold in explaining why these particular things happened. They happened as examples from which others could learn. Do not let your experiences go unnoticed. Learn from others also. You are not the first person to go through your situation. Learn the easy way! The hard way will end up killing you. It is crazy for you to make the same mistake you have seen in others. Learn from them. Look for people who are walking with the Lord and learn from them, too.

From this same section of verses 1 Corinthians 10:13 says, *"No temptation has overtaken you that is not common to man. God is faithful, and he will not let you be tempted beyond your ability, but with the temptation he will also provide the way of escape, that you may be able to endure it."* God is faithful. He will not let you down. His mercies are new every morning. He loves you so much. He wants you to trust Him. He desires to deliver you. When you are weak, He will be strong if you cry out to Him. Only God can deliver you; He will provide a way for you to escape.

Mood alternating substances are all drugs. When it controls you, it will be there at every turn just waiting to take you down. God will provide a way out for you, but it is going to take hard work, determination, faith, prayer, fasting, being around godly people, and reading God's Word. God's way of escape is a choice only you can make.

The hard way is nowhere. Learn from your past and the mistakes of others. Ask God, "Lead me not into temptation, deliver me from evil." Surround yourself with God's ways, people, His Word, and whatsoever things are beneficial, right, and honorable. Think on these ideas.

"You can't do it, but it can be done" sounds like an oxymoron kind of statement. But it will make sense when you give your life to Jesus and choose to walk in His ways.

What have you learned from your own experiences?

_____
_____
_____
_____

42

RUNNING SCARED

We have all experienced fear, even if just for a moment. It is that instance when our breath is taken away because of what might happen to us physically or even emotionally. One would think the fear of death (thanatophobia) would be the strongest fear, but it has been said that people fear public speaking more than death (glossophobia). It is interesting that the fear of emotional danger might be more intense than that of physical danger. Some statistics state that the fear of spiders (arachnophobia) is the most common fear of all. I am not sure if that is more of a physical fear or emotional. Acrophobia (the fear of heights) and claustrophobia (fear of enclosed spaces) have been fears that people have admitted for years. In recent times, there have been other fears that have been voiced like coulrophobia (the fear of clowns) and nomophobia (the fear of being out of mobile phone service). What fear is hippopotomonstrosesquippedaliophobia? The most natural guess is the fear of some large animal. However, it is the fear of long words. Hopefully, it will not be on the list for the next Spelling Bee or your opponent's next Scrabble word. I am not sure how many points a 36 letter word that has a 'q' in it would be worth.

Fear, no matter how silly it appears, can cause us to freeze or flee. David may have conquered Goliath, but he too experienced fear.

He writes about one instance in Psalm 55. Verses 5-8 say, *"Fear and trembling come upon me, and horror overwhelms me. And I say, 'Oh, that I had wings like a dove! I would fly away and be at rest; yes, I would wander far away; I would lodge in the wilderness; Selah. I would hurry to find a shelter from the raging wind and tempest.'"* David, the giant killer, now wishes he could fly away, find shelter to hide, or just run. He is paralyzed with fear. It consumes his thoughts. Fear can come from danger or emotions. You might be fearful because of hidden sin coming out, that you will use again, or that family and friends will never trust you again. Unfortunately, fear makes false evidence appear real.

In the addiction world running is important. You need to run from sin and run to God.

1. Run from sin. Hebrews 12:1-2 says, *"Therefore, since we are surrounded by so great a cloud of witnesses, let us also lay aside every weight, and sin which clings so closely, and let us run with endurance the race that is set before us."* Drop your sin. Sin will weigh you down. Addiction holds you back. Do not run from help. 1 Corinthians 6:18 adds, *"Flee from sexual immorality. Every other sin a person commits is outside the body, but the sexually immoral person sins against his own body."* Flee means to run from it. Sin does not cover sin. It builds up higher and higher. Guilt is a negative motivator. It is a vicious cycle. Whatever causes you to use, lay that weight aside. If that weight is guilt, lay it aside. It will consume you. It will lock you up inside. Jesus sets the captives free.

2 Timothy 2:22 talks about fleeing again, *"So flee youthful passions and pursue righteousness, faith, love, and peace, along with those who call on the Lord from a pure heart."* Flee sin; run to Christ. He is the only answer.

2. Run to God. Psalm 31:1 says, *"In you, O Lord, do I take refuge; let me never be put to shame; in your righteousness deliver me!"* The Message Bible paraphrases it as, *"I run to you, God; I run for dear life. Don't let me down! Take me seriously this time!"* Run with endurance and patience. Run the race towards freedom. Man up and get some endurance. Tough it out day by day. Do not run away from God. Face your issues. See the light.

May 27th is 'Nothing to Fear Day,' while October 13th is 'Face Your Fears Day.' How can you face your fears if there is nothing to fear? Also, what if the October 13th day lands on a Friday? Is that a double negative and hence positive?

We can joke about fears and phobias, but they do play a role in your life. Fear causes people to run. Make sure you know why you are running. You are either running from something, to something, or both. I hope it is both in that you are running from sin and to God.

Does fear have you running in the wrong direction?

_____

_____

_____

What steps do you need to take to run toward God?

_____

_____

_____

_____

_____

_____

43

LIAR, LIAR, PANTS ON FIRE

There is a fun riddle on lying: You are on a journey and come to a fork in the road. There are two men standing there. You have been warned by a friend that the one man always tells the truth and the other man always lies. However, you do not know which one always tells the truth or which one always lies. You need to know which path to take, and you only get one question. What would you ask? If you ask, "Which path am I to take?" They will point in opposite directions, and you will not see which one is right. The correct question is to ask them, "Which direction would the other man say I should go?" When you get their answer go in the opposite direction because the liar will lie and tell you the wrong way and the truthful man will tell you the lie that the liar would say.

Addicts are known for being liars. It has been said that you can always tell when an addict is lying, his or her lips are moving.

Liars have to have a good memory. You have to remember what story you told each person. You become trapped in your lies. Sadly, you lie for the sake of lying. Eventually, you start to believe your lies. You lie to yourself.

In John 8:30-33 Jesus challenges a group of religious people, *"As he was saying these things, many believed in him. So Jesus said to the Jews who had believed him, 'If you abide in my word, you are truly my disciples, and you will know the truth, and the truth will set you free.' They answered him, 'We are offspring of Abraham and have never been enslaved to anyone. How is it that you say, 'You will become free?'"* Too many people believe that religion will save them. Religion tends to become a system that focuses too much on us. Jesus was offering a relationship, a relationship with God Himself. Jesus was sharing the truth and offering freedom, but these prideful men fell back on their religion. Their religion did not bring satisfaction or peace, but they convinced themselves it was the answer.

Jesus told them to speak the truth and live the truth. He was interested in their talk and their walk. Addicts play a game. They talk one way, but live another. They tend to perfect the art of lying to others and even themselves. Addicts play the denial game. Their life can be summarized in the acronym G-A-M-E.

1. You <u>give</u> glory to yourself. You cannot beat addiction yourself. Only Jesus can do it. Philippians 4:13 clearly states, *"I can do all things through him who strengthens me."* Paul knew he could succeed with Jesus, but he could not do it alone.

2. You <u>act</u> like something that you are not. Quit faking it. Stop playing the game; it can kill you. Be honest with yourself. Be honest with God. Be honest with others. Ephesians 4:25 says, *"Therefore, having put away falsehood, let each one of you speak the truth with his neighbor, for we are members one of another."*

3. You <u>make</u> what others think more important than it is. Do not worry about what others say about you. Haters will hate. Your focus should be on God. 2 Timothy 2:15 says, *"Do your best to present yourself to God as one approved, a worker who has no need to be ashamed, rightly handling the word of truth."* Focus on what God thinks. Focus on pleasing God.

4. You <u>elect</u> to lie to self. The addiction 'game' is a con-game. You con yourself and then others. You lie to yourself that you do not have a problem. You lie to yourself that you can stop anytime you want. You lie to yourself that you do not need anyone's help. You start with small lies, and then it grows. It even becomes a game. Albert Einstein said, "Whoever is careless with the truth in small matters cannot be trusted with important matters." Be honest with yourself. Remember, *"The truth will set you free."* Quit playing the 'game;' declare 'Game Over.'

The addiction world is based on a foundation of lies. Beating addiction can only happen through living a life of truth. You can't do it, but it can be done. What seems IMPOSSIBLE, has followers of Jesus saying I M POSSIBLE!

How would you summarize your conversations, your talk?

_____

_____

_____

How would you summarize your lifestyle, your walk?

_____

_____

_____

_____

_____

44

A STINKY SOLUTION

I n 2010 David Haviland wrote a book entitled, *Why You Should Store Your Farts in a Jar*. That is the craziest title ever. It is a book about some of the odd and gross things people did thinking it would help or heal them:

- Egyptians use to put dead mice in their mouth to cure a toothache.
- As recent as a couple of hundred years ago, doctors would cut off half of the tongue of someone who stuttered.
- Egyptians would use moldy bread to disinfect cuts.
- During the Middle Ages doctors had to face Black Death. They tried to fight the deadly vapor by having patients find something else to smell. They encouraged 'Farts in a Jar.'

When you have a disease or sickness, you can get to the point when you would try almost anything. Addicts have a sickness. You may have been born with an addiction, followed the example of someone older, or just went out on your own and started down the road to destruction. It seemed like a harmless thrill, but now it owns you. It is a sickness.

The Bible talks about a horrible disease called leprosy. It is noticed for sores on your skin appearing to kill the skin, but its most destructive element is the nerve damage. It was believed to be highly contagious, so an infected individual became an outcast of society. They had to yell, "Unclean, unclean" anytime someone came near them.

One guy in particular in the Bible that had leprosy was Naaman. 2 Kings 5:1 says, *"Naaman, commander of the army of the king of Syria, was a great man with his master and in high favor, because by him the Lord had given victory to Syria. He was a mighty man of valor, but he was a leper."* There are four things you can learn from Naaman's life and sickness.

1. Realize you have a problem. The passage tells us that Naaman was a leper. Even though he was a mighty man, he stilled knew he was a leper. If you do not realize you have a problem, you will not put in the effort to correct it. Problems do not heal themselves.

2. Identify the enemy. 2 Kings 5 has a real twist in it, *"Now the Syrians on one of their raids had carried off a little girl from the land of Israel, and she worked in the service of Naaman's wife. 3 She said to her mistress, "Would that my lord were with the prophet who is in Samaria! He would cure him of his leprosy"* (verse 2-3). This girl was kidnapped from her family and still helps her master. It is interesting that she realized that the disease was the real enemy. The Church needs to know that addiction, not addicts, is the enemy. Satan rules the addiction world and the Church needs to know he is the enemy. God loves addicts and so should we. You are amazing. Realize you have a problem and remember who the enemy is. There are people in your life who want to help.

3. Be willing to do whatever is necessary. Elisha was an amazing man of God. God did several miracles through Elisha. 2 Kings 5:10-12 says, *"And Elisha sent a messenger to him, saying, 'Go and wash in the Jordan seven times, and your flesh shall be restored, and you shall be clean.' But Naaman was angry and went away, saying, 'Behold, I thought that he would surely come out to me and stand and call upon the name of the Lord his God, and wave his hand over the place and cure the leper. Are not Abana and Pharpar, the rivers of Damascus, better than all the waters of Israel? Could I not wash in them and be clean?' So he turned and went away in a rage."* To beat addiction, you need God and faith. Naaman knew he had a problem. It crippled him every day, yet when he is told what he needs to do, he refuses. It does sound crazy to wash in a river seven times, but faith takes action. It should also be noted that Naaman raided Elisha's people, but Elisha did not view Naaman as an enemy. The disease is the enemy.

2 Kings 5:13-14 continues the story, *"But his servants came near and said to him, 'My father, it is a great word the prophet has spoken to you; will you not do it? Has he actually said to you, 'Wash, and be clean?' So he went down and dipped himself seven times in the Jordan, according to the word of the man of God, and his flesh was restored like the flesh of a little child, and he was clean."* Finally, Naaman steps out in faith. He washes in the Jordan and is healed. The water was not the cure. Faith in God followed by action brought success.

4. Give God the glory. Naaman was not a man of God. He was not a religious man. However, 2 Kings 5:15 says, *"Then he returned to the man of God, he and all his company, and he came and stood before him. And he said, 'Behold, I know* *that there is no God in all the earth but in Israel; so accept now a present from your servant.'"* Naaman was healed. He did not take the credit. He gave God the glory. You need to be healed from addiction. You can't do it, but it can be done. It can only be done through Jesus Christ.

What is your sickness?

_____

_____

_____

_____

What is the next step of faith God wants you to take?

_____

_____

_____

_____

_____

_____

45

SHIPSHAPE

It has been said, "The best two days in a boater's life is the day he buys it, and the day he sells it." It appears there is a time when ownership changes. At first, you own the boat. Later, the boat and all the maintenance owns you.

Boat owners love talking about their vessel. *All Things Boats* lists some creative, witty, and funny actual ship names:

- Dock Holiday
- A-Loan at Last
- Pier Pressure
- Reel Time
- The Salt Shaker
- Vitamin Sea

Although boat owning has some high points, there are stories of how things can go really bad. In Acts 27 Paul, the prisoner, is traveling by way of a ship when the weather turns sour. Verse 27 describes what is happening as they are trying to ride out the storm, ***"When the fourteenth night had come, as we were being driven across the Adriatic Sea, about midnight the sailors suspected that they were nearing land."***

Paul is being transported to Rome to face trial. He is on a ship when a storm sets in. The crew is terrified and panicked. He is on the ship, and when the fourteenth day had come, at midnight the sailors thought they were near land. They found the depth to be 20 fathoms and then 15. The sailors threw the anchors off the back to put the brakes on as they feared smashing into the rocks. Some of the sailors tried to abandon ship by leaving on a small boat. Paul warned them that they would not survive. The Roman soldiers cut the line to the small boat.

The addiction world will destroy your life. You need to talk straight about life's battles. You are on the sea of life and are in dire trouble. Figure out where you are.

When you are going through a storm and about to crash, you should ask two questions.

1. Why am I where I am? You could also ask, "Why is this happening?" Be honest with yourself. Evaluate your life. In what storms have you put yourself? Do not blame others. Own your life.

You also need to honestly answer whether or not you are an addict. If you are using every day, you are an addict. If you do not want to use, but you do anyway, you are an addict. If you have been arrested for it, or it has cost you your family or job, you are an addict. God wants you to experience an incredible life with an amazing Savior.

2. Who should I talk to? Most people think they need to ask, "What should I do?" First, talk to people whom will be honest with you. Sometimes it may not be your family. You can't do it, but it can be done. Your life's ship will hit the rocks unless you get

real and honest with yourself. Hit the brakes before you hit the rocks. Stop! Stop! Addicts often say, "I am going to stop when..." Hit the brakes. Stop now. Every day using takes you deeper into trouble.

Be careful with whom you hang out. The sailors bailed out on Paul and the passengers. Your 'friends' will bail out on you when the dope runs out. Continuous using is a death sentence. It is not a game. You will never win the addiction game; you will lose. The Centurions cut loose the lifeboats. It was a drastic situation. You need to make a drastic decision to save your life. Your choice might be to not carry any money so you cannot buy any stuff. You might choose to change with whom you hang out. The party group is no longer your trusted friends. They might not be bad people, but when you are with them bad things happen. You might choose to change your regular routine or route. There are streets and corners you need to avoid.

You are meant to sail an amazing life. One of my favorite boat names is Seas the Day. It is a play on the phrase 'Seize the day.' In the movie Dead Poets Society, the teacher, Robin Williams, uses a Latin phrase with his students – 'carpe diem.' It means to seize the day or make the most of today. God has a plan for your life. Changes need to be made. Start today! Seas the Day!

Who should you talk to?

_____

_____

What changes do you need to make?

_____

_____

_____

46

S-T-O-P

*S*tormforce *Coaching* is a boating website that includes many boating puns:

- I used to have a fear of boats, but that ship has sailed!
- Making a boat out of stone would be a hardship!
- In ancient times, seagoing vessels were much more efficient. They got thousands of miles to the galleon!
- A ship's captain is a sails manager!
- The admiral's motto was, 'Do it schooner rather than later!'

It reminds me of the old silly joke: How much did it cost the pirate to get his ears pierced? A Buccaneer (A buck an ear)!

Puns or 'a play on words' can be fun. Teasing about boats is okay, but when you are headed for the rocks, it is no joking matter. The last chapter introduced us to a shipping experience that Paul was experiencing. The storm was creating a helpless situation. A shipwreck was inevitable. This chapter will continue to look at Acts 27 to see what else can be learned that will help addicts. The acronym S – T – O – P may help you memorize the steps needed to 'STOP' addiction.

1. Spiritual Leadership is essential. Acts 27:33-40 says, *"As day was about to dawn, Paul urged them all to take some food, saying, 'Today is the fourteenth day that you have continued in suspense and without food, having taken nothing. Therefore I urge you to take some food. For it will give you strength, for not a hair is to perish from the head of any of you.' And when he had said these things, he took bread, and giving thanks to God in the presence of all he broke it and began to eat. Then they all were encouraged and ate some food themselves. (We were in all 276 persons in the ship.)"* Paul is now in a leadership position. He is a prisoner headed for the rocks, yet he takes charge, and people listen. It is a large group, and he steps up. Proverbs 15:22 says, *"Without counsel plans fail, but with many advisers they succeed."* We need each other. Ask others for advice. Get godly advice.

Be careful with whom you listen. Just because someone says they are godly or has a title like a pastor, priest, or minister, does not mean they will give good advice. Some of these 'leaders' only point people to themselves. You need someone who will lead you to God. Strength will come from the Word of God.

2. Throw stuff overboard. Verse 38 continues the story, *"And when they had eaten enough, they lightened the ship, throwing out the wheat into the sea."* After listening to good advice, they threw stuff overboard. Do not carry extra baggage. Get rid of junk that weighs you down. Dispose of the anger, bitterness, hatred, and guilt. Lighten your load physically, mentally, emotionally, and spiritually. Pull up your anchors and move forward. God created you to be amazing. Be all that God wants you to be.

3. Optimism helps. Verse 39 adds, *"Now when it was day, they did not recognize the land, but they noticed a bay with a beach, on which they planned if possible to run the ship ashore."* The sailors see land and feel there is hope. Hope can drive us. Jesus Christ brings hope. He makes the impossible, possible.

4. Plans are necessary. Finally, verses 39-40 say, *"Now when it was day, they did not recognize the land, but they noticed a bay with a beach, on which they planned if possible to run the ship ashore. So they cast off the anchors and left them in the sea, at the same time loosening the ropes that tied the rudders. Then hoisting the foresail to the wind they made for the beach."* The sailors found a place and formed a plan to beach the boat. You need to get a plan.

God designed you to be something. Become what God wants you to be. God has an abundant life for you. Have this motto for life: You can either sit it out, or you can dance. Addiction makes you sit it out. Stop the addiction. Learn to dance. Learn to enjoy life. Live a life blessed by God.

Spiritual leadership – who is helpful in directing in the right direction?

_____

_____

Throw – what do you need to get rid of?

_____

_____

_____

_____

Optimism – what is something good that you see happening soon?

_____

_____

_____

_____

Plans – what is your game plan? What are your next few steps?

_____

_____

_____

_____

_____

_____

47

OBITUARY

Have you ever thought what your obituary would say? Alfred Nobel read his obituary. No, he had not died yet. It was a mistake. His brother had died, but the newspaper thought it was him and wrote on how much death and destruction he had caused by inventing dynamite. He was floored. He immediately changed his life. He put forth all his time, energy, and resources in bringing peace to others. He started focusing on how to help others. To help encourage such actions he created the Nobel Peace Prize.

What will it take to change your life? If you think you have already arrived, you are in a dangerous place. It all begins with your mindset. Your thoughts will become your actions. Your actions become your legacy. Whatever you are facing today, God has provided an amazing way for you to live a fulfilled life. It begins with your mind. Think about what you are thinking about.

In Philippians 4:8 Paul says, *"Finally, brothers, whatever is true, whatever is honorable, whatever is just, whatever is pure, whatever is lovely, whatever is commendable, if there is any excellence, if there is anything worthy of praise, think about these things."* Paul tells them to 'think' about these things. Think! Think before you do! Take inventory in your life and then do the things you are supposed to do. God has big plans for you if you can make the adjustments in your life.

There are four questions to ask when evaluating what you are thinking about.

1. What is there? Take inventory. You might be afraid to take an honest look at your life. If you are an angry person, you will always find someone who makes you mad. If you are a person of love, you will always find someone to love. Paul continues in Philippians 4:9 saying, *"What you have learned and received and heard and seen in me—practice these things, and the God of peace will be with you."* See what is in your life and then look at the life of someone you respect who is following God. Then figure out what you need to do. Paul encouraged people to follow his example. Be honest with yourself. Make a change. Get yourself out of bad influences and get yourself into a group that will help you do what you need to do.

2. What is not there? What is missing in your life? Romans 12:2 also speaks about how we think, *"Do not be conformed to this world, but be transformed by the renewal of your mind, that by testing you may discern what is the will of God, what is good and acceptable and perfect."* Figure out what is missing in your life and do something about it. If you are missing things like love and honesty, then start thinking differently. Choose to show love to other people by smiling, saying kind words, and helping with different projects. Set your mind on being honest. Refuse to lie or deceive. Be truthful.

3. What is not needed? Ephesians 4:22-24 also challenges our thinking, *"You were taught, with regard to your former way* *of life, to put off your old self, which is being corrupted by its deceitful desires; to be made new in the attitude of your minds; and to put on the new self, created to be like God in true righteousness and holiness"* (NIV). Here Paul says you are to *"put off your old self"* get a *"new in the attitude of your minds,"* and *"put on the new self."* If you want to be a new person, it starts with the mind. Proper thinking helps you change from your old self to being a new and improved man. Figure out what is not needed. Look on the shelf of your life and see what has gone wrong. Toss out the areas of your life that are bad and rotten.

4. What is needed? When you eliminate something from your life, you need to fill it with something better. Galatians 5:22-23 gives a perfect list, *"But the fruit of the Spirit is love, joy, peace, patience, kindness, goodness, faithfulness, gentleness, self-control; against such things there is no law."* This is what should be in your life. It is the Fruit of the Spirit. Think about positive things. Think of good things.

It is not enjoyable to think about our funeral or obituary, but it can be helpful. In Matthew 25:23 Jesus says, *"His master said to him, 'Well done, good and faithful servant. You have been faithful over a little; I will set you over much. Enter into the joy of your master.'"* Those are the words you should want to hear, *"Well done, good and faithful servant."*

197

What do you want your obituary to say?

_____

_____

_____

_____

What do you need to do to start making that happen?

_____

_____

_____

_____

48

POUR IT ON

P eople can come across as know-it-alls. *Stories for Preaching* lists several predictions people made in pride that proved to be very false:

- In 1876, a Western Union internal memo said, "This 'telephone' has too many shortcomings to be seriously considered as a means of communication. The device is inherently of no value to us." Today most people will not leave home without their phone. Some family members even text each other while they are both home.
- Irving Fisher, a professor of Economics at Yale University, said, "Stocks have reached what looks like a permanently high plateau." He said this in 1929 right before the market crash and the Great Depression.
- As recent as 1977, Ken Olson, president of Digital Equipment Corporation said, "There is no reason anyone would want a computer in their home."
- Gary Cooper said, "I'm just glad it'll be Clark Gable who's falling on his face and not Gary Cooper." Cooper said this right after he made his decision not to take the leading role in Gone With The Wind.

- Finally, Decca Recording Company said, "We don't like their sound, and guitar music is on the way out." It was 1962, and they had just rejected a group called 'The Beatles.'

There have always been people who make very dogmatic statements. They say something, and they come across as if they are a know-it-all. Their pride becomes their downfall. It is funny to go back and see how wrong they were.

Pride can be a major problem for addicts. You say you do not need any help. You yell that you can stop anytime you want. You try to convince family and friends that using will not change you. You brag that you will not get caught. This pride takes you down. The Bible says a lot on the topic of pride.

"When pride comes, then comes disgrace, but with the humble is wisdom." Proverbs 11:2

"Pride goes before destruction, and a haughty spirit before a fall." Proverbs 16:18

"One's pride will bring him low, but he who is lowly in spirit will obtain honor." Proverbs 29:23

"But he gives more grace. Therefore it says, "God opposes the proud but gives grace to the humble."" James 4:6

Pride brings people down to destruction. However, having a lowly spirit and humility puts us in the position where God will bless. Pride puts us in a situation in which it appears we feel we do not need God. It is as if He steps away from us and stops holding us up. We fall. On the other hand, there are those you realize they need God. He reaches down from Heaven and lifts them up. God resists the proud, but gives grace to the humble.

How does God help you? Grace is God working with you. God shows up in your life. Whatever you are fighting, God's grace can always abound. Pride says, "I can do it; I do not need any help." Humility says, "I cannot do it alone." Lose the pride; take the humility, wisdom, and grace.

God does not enjoy watching the prideful fall. He wants to see humility and then pour out His grace. John 1:16 takes it to another level, *"For from his fullness we have all received, grace upon grace."* It is the difference between getting a scoop of ice cream (which is good) and getting an extra scoop with any toppings you want (hot fudge, cool whip, nuts, and the cherry). That is even better. God wants to pour it on. He desires to give us grace and then pour on some more. God wants to pour it on.

God gives grace when you realize who you are. We all struggle. You will never be fixed until you understand you are broken. It is not how you do what you do. It is how you ask God to do what only God can do.

In what ways is your pride hurting you?

_____

_____

_____

How can you become more humble (humbler)?

_____

_____

_____

_____

49

USEFUL

"I get paid peanuts." That is usually not intended as a positive statement. The history of the statement is unsure, but peanuts have been around for a long time and have always been viewed as having little value. When flying, I have not heard much excitement about peanuts replacing a meal. Peanuts? Are not those for the zoo? Do we not snack on them at certain restaurants and throw the shells on the floor? Peanuts? Do they have any value?

George Washington Carver is one of my heroes. He did not give up on something based on outward appearance. He took the peanut to an incredible level. He created some 300 uses for the "valueless" peanut. He made things like peanut sausage, caramel, mayonnaise, coffee, shampoo, shaving cream, glue, rubber, and even nitroglycerine. That is the bomb!

Sometimes people feel like they are valueless or are not useful. This can be a common problem for addicts and inmates. The Bible has several books that were written by Paul while he was in prison. He writes Colossians and Philemon while behind bars. They are books of encouragement. They remind us that Paul and Pastors like him even need help from time to tome. Tychicus is hardly ever mentioned in the Bible, but he is a friend and helper of Paul.

Colossians 4:7-9 says, *"Tychicus will tell you all about my activities. He is a beloved brother and faithful minister and fellow servant in the Lord. I have sent him to you for this very purpose, that you may know how we are and that he may encourage your hearts, and with him Onesimus, our faithful and beloved brother, who is one of you. They will tell you of everything that has taken place here."* Paul wanted Tychicus to share with Philemon and his friends at the church at Colossae exactly who Paul was and what he was experiencing. Tychicus understood Paul and Paul could trust him. It is hard for Pastors to trust others. Unfortunately, rumors can abound. Things people say can affect Pastors and their families. Pastors need sound men to come alongside them. Men who know them, will stand up for them, and can be counted on for support. Be a man of God. Put others first, be faithful, get character and integrity like Tychicus. Be a fellow servant.

Paul also mentioned Onesimus to the people at Colossae. Paul calls Onesimus *"our faithful and beloved brother."* Paul lets us know more about him in Philemon 1:10-12, *"I appeal to you for my child, Onesimus, whose father I became in my imprisonment. (Formerly he was useless to you, but now he is indeed useful to you and to me.) I am sending him back to you, sending my very heart."* The rest of the story tells us that Onesimus was a runaway slave who stole from others and ends up in prison with Paul. Philemon was his owner. Paul writes Philemon to forgive Onesimus. Paul goes on to say that formerly Onesimus *"was useless to you, but now he is indeed useful to you and to me."* Onesimus changed his life. He used to be selfish and self-serving. He did not have such a great life. He did not have reason to be proud. He was a mess. He was of no value or use to others. He changed. Now he was useful to Paul and to others. Onesimus turned from himself and looked to Jesus. He gave his life to Jesus, got connected with others who followed Jesus, and started serving. He became a man of action.

A deeper study brings some humor to the story. The name 'Onesimus' means 'useful.' Think about it; 'Useful' used to be 'useless' to Philemon, but was 'useful' to Paul and would be 'useful' to Philemon in the future. Change your reputation. Be Onesimus. Be useful.

Take a moment the next time you are at a restaurant that has peanuts on the table. As you snack on a few and throw the shells on the ground (that was so fun as a kid), remember Dr. Carver filled a grocery list with them. Also, remember that outward appearance can be deceptive. Little things and 'forgotten' people like addicts and inmates are valuable and can be useful.

Everyone you see today has value (even the person in the mirror)!

Can your pastor or chaplain count on you?

_____

_____

Who else needs your help today?

_____

_____

_____

_____

50

FIT TO BE TIED

Have you ever seen someone get so mad that they punched a wall? They typically end up with a sprained or broken hand without anything changing that made them angry. If you plan on hitting a wall, I encourage you to calculate from the end of the wall at sixteen-inch increments so that you only punch the drywall and not the stud. You can defeat drywall, but studs frequently hurt. By the way, your anger will still be there or even worse, you will have medical bills, you will have a hard time working to pay those bills, and you will end up with a remodeling project.

Have you ever seen someone get so mad that they punched a locker? It does not help. Hopefully, they estimated where the shelf is behind the locker, so they do not hit reinforced metal. By the way, if you plan on punching a door, make sure it is hollow and is not reinforced with a metal plate on the backside.

Anger often plays a significant role in the addiction world. The detox center strives to help you get rid of your addiction physically. It is not as easy to detox your emotions. When things start going crazy, emotions kick in and can drive you to use. Triggers can set your emotions. Anger is one of those triggers. Most people have issues with anger. There are three questions that should be addressed when discussing anger.

1. Is anger sin? Anger is not sin; it is a God-given emotion. Jesus got angry in the synagogue and turned over the tables of the money changers. He was mad, but He did not sin. Ephesians 4:26 says, *"Be angry and do not sin; do not let the sun go down on your anger."* Check out the first two words, *"Be angry."* Anger is not always wrong. It is not automatically sin. It tells us that there are times when being angry is necessary and right, but to be careful, you do not get out of control. People in your life can press the buttons that tend to stir up your emotions, but remember, emotions are a choice. Anger is a choice. Sin is a choice; it is a wrong choice.

2. What can anger cost you? Uncontrolled anger can cost you. Moses grew up in the king's house and one day saw an Egyptian beating an Israelite. He stepped in, but in the process killed the Egyptian. This act cost Moses. He had to spend the next forty years in the wilderness because of his unrighteous anger.

Eventually, Moses led the people of Israel out of Egypt. They were wandering in the wilderness when they started to complain that they had no water. God answers their cry in Exodus 17:6, *"'Behold, I will stand before you there on the rock at Horeb, and you shall strike the rock, and water shall come out of it, and the people will drink.' And Moses did so, in the sight of the elders of Israel."* God tells Moses to strike the rock. Moses struck the rock and water poured out of the rock. All the people had plenty to drink. Later, they are in a similar situation of not having water. God gives Moses instructions in Numbers 20:8, *"Take the staff, and assemble the congregation, you and Aaron your brother, and tell the rock before their eyes to yield its water. So you shall bring water out of the rock for them and give drink to the congregation and their cattle."* Did you notice the difference? This time God tells Moses to speak to the rock and water will pour out. He does not tell him to hit the rock. Moses is angry. He disobeys God. He blasts the rock. God still sends water, but He remembered Moses' sin. As a result, God did not let Moses enter the Promised Land. God forgave Moses, but his sin still had consequences.

You can get angry with other people, but be careful. Sometimes the only person it hurts is yourself. Do not lose your temper. It can put you in the same place as Moses, killing someone. The consequences are not good. Moses was a man who spent time with God but appeared to have anger issues. Even when God gave him the Ten Commandments, Moses got angry at the sin of the people and threw them down. He broke all Ten Commandments in just two seconds (it might be a record). He then had to go back and ask God to rewrite them. That would have been embarrassing. It would have been an awkward moment.

3. What will you do about anger? Anger can be used for good or evil. It can be right or wrong. It can help or hurt. The women of Israel came to Nehemiah and explained how they were done wrong. His response is found in Nehemiah 5:6, *"I was very angry when I heard their outcry and these words."* Nehemiah was angry. You can always get angry at someone or something. Sinful anger is hard to conquer. Nehemiah's response comes in the very next verse, *"I took counsel with myself, and I brought charges against the nobles and the officials. I said to them, 'You are exacting interest, each from his brother.' And I held a great assembly against them."* Nehemiah paused and consulted with himself. Ask yourself questions. Look into the future. Will anger fix the issue or just confound things. Do not immediately react to

your emotions. Anger out of control can lead to using. Seek God. He will not tell you to use.

What areas are anger hurting you?

_____
_____
_____
_____
_____
_____

In what areas are you right in voicing your anger?

_____
_____
_____
_____
_____
_____

51

REACH

There are stories regularly reported when fishermen need to be rescued. Sports Illustrated reported a story where Lucas Patchen, a high school basketball player in New York, was benched for his game because he missed the team bus. He was late because he was with volunteer firemen who were rescuing an ice fisherman from Lake Ontario. He could not contact anyone because of the actions needed in helping. He was viewed as a hero but was benched for the game.

Most people are familiar with Jesus walking on water, but they miss the part where Peter walks on water, and Jesus needs to rescue this sinking fisherman. Matthew 14:28-31 says, *"And Peter answered him, 'Lord, if it is you, command me to come to you on the water.' He said, 'Come.' So Peter got out of the boat and walked on the water and came to Jesus. But when he saw the wind, he was afraid, and beginning to sink he cried out, 'Lord, save me.' Jesus immediately reached out his hand and took hold of him, saying to him, 'O you of little faith, why did you doubt?'"* Jesus is walking on water when He approaches the disciples who are in their boat. They are panicked due to weather and seeing someone or something approaching them. They are over three miles away from shore and think they see things. Jesus identifies Himself, so Peter asks for proof; he asks to walk on water. He steps out of the boat. He is doing well for awhile, but then he starts to sink. There are three things to note from what happens next in this passage.

1. Call out to God. Peter is sinking, and he asks for help. Peter is a fisherman and was raised on the water. He could swim. Scripture shares other times when he jumps out of the boat even though he is some ways from shore. It would be natural for him to act as if he could handle it all by himself. He could have remained silent so he would not be embarrassed in front of his friends, the other disciples. He knew he was in trouble. He asked God for help. Jesus saved him.

Addicts need to ask for help. You need to ask God to help you. God will not give up on you. He loves you. He wants to help. He sees you sinking and is waiting for you to ask Him to help you. Do not let your pride of image get in the way. You cannot be helped until you realize your need. You cannot do it, but it can be done.

2. God will reach out to you. Picture Jesus and Peter on the water as you read, *"Jesus immediately reached out his hand and took hold of him."* Jesus reached down and pulled Peter to safety. David was not walking on water, but he could relate to being saved by God. In Psalm 138:6-7 he says, *"For though the Lord is high, he regards the lowly, but the haughty he knows from afar. Though I walk in the midst of trouble, you preserve my life; you stretch out your hand against the wrath of my enemies, and your right hand delivers me."* I picture Jesus holding back the enemy and danger with His left hand while rescuing me with His strong right hand. He sees your need. When you call out to Him, He will reach out to you.

David was a shepherd, not a fisherman. However, he also experienced God's saving hand. In Psalm 23:4 he says, *"Even though I walk through the valley of the shadow of death, I will fear no evil, for you are with me; your rod and your staff, they comfort me."* David knew the danger. He was in situations that were out of his control. He could have run. He could have given up. Instead, he looked to God. He was comforted by the fact that God was with him.

3. Give your life to God. Trust Him. Take His hand. Peter called out to Jesus, and Jesus immediately reached out to him. Peter had a choice. Peter could ignore the help, or he could totally trust his Savior and take His hand. He chose to put his life into the hand of Jesus. Jesus did not give up on him. He had big plans for him. Peter is an instrumental leader in the early Church. He was used in mighty ways by God.

Going back to Psalm 138, David writes in verse 8, *"The Lord will fulfill his purpose for me; your steadfast love, O Lord, endures forever. Do not forsake the work of your hands."* God will fulfill His purpose for you. He will not give up on the works of His hands. Your life has value, meaning, and a purpose. God has a plan for your life. He will not give up on you. God's mercy never runs out. God made you; He does not make junk. God is reaching out to you. Take His hand. Trust Him. Give Him your life.

When troubles come, you have a choice. You can sink in despair, or you can cry out to God. You can keep doing it your way and destroy your life and those around you, or you can see God reaching out to you. You can run and try to escape life through drugs, a bottle, and using or you can find peace and hope by giving your life to God. Jesus is reaching out to you; take His hand. Let Him lead you to a blessed life.

What is your biggest struggle right now?

_____

_____

_____

_____

_____

_____

How can God help? Talk to Him.

_____

_____

_____

_____

_____

_____

_____

_____

_____

_____

_____

52

RECOVERY

People get stuck in some of the strangest places. *ODDEE* reports "oddities, weird stuff, and strange things of the world." They have accumulated several scenarios where people got stuck.

- In China, eighteen people got stuck on a roller coaster for thirty minutes. That does not sound horrible until you realize they were stuck upside down.
- They report a man whose arm got stuck in a toilet. He dropped his phone in the toilet, and as he tried to retrieve it, his arm got stuck.
- A three-year-old was playing an arcade game where you direct the claw to pick up a prize. He wanted a prize so bad that he climbed into the prize shoot. The door closed behind, and he was stuck inside.
- One lady got stuck in an elevator for three days, and another lady got locked in her bathroom for three weeks. Neither one sounds fun.
- Finally, a man tried to break into a pizza place by climbing through the air shafts. He got stuck in the vent and screamed for help for about thirty minutes.

It can be funny to hear people who get stuck, especially when it is their fault. However, being stuck is not any fun. If you have ever been stuck, felt claustrophobic, or living in a rut, you understand the overwhelming sensation of feeling there is no way out.

Jeremiah writes about his experience of despair in Jeremiah 38. He warns the people of coming destruction, and instead of giving their life to the Lord, they get mad at him. Verse 6 says, *"So they took Jeremiah and cast him into the cistern of Malchiah, the king's son, which was in the court of the guard, letting Jeremiah down by ropes. And there was no water in the cistern, but only mud and Jeremiah sank in the mud."* They threw Jeremiah in a dried up cistern, a pit, a hole in the ground. He was stuck, trapped, and left alone. They did not have a cell, so they threw him in a well.

Ebed-melech knew that Jeremiah was done wrong, so he went to the king asking if he could help. The king gave him permission to rescue Jeremiah. Verses 11-13 say, *"So Ebed-melech took the men with him and went to the house of the king, to a wardrobe in the storehouse, and took from there old rags and worn-out clothes, which he let down to Jeremiah in the cistern by ropes. Then Ebed-melech the Ethiopian said to Jeremiah, 'Put the rags and clothes between your armpits and the ropes.' Jeremiah did so. Then they drew Jeremiah up with ropes and lifted him out of the cistern. And Jeremiah remained in the court of the guard."* This passage gives three clear principles that relate to your life today.

1. God sends people to help rescue you. Jeremiah was alone. It appeared that he would starve to death in this pit, but God sent someone. God sent Ebed-melech to rescue Jeremiah. He was stuck in a mess, and God sent help. Are you stuck in a mess? Have you found yourself in the bottom of a pit, in the stench and filth? Jeremiah was trying to figure out how to get out, and God sent someone.

2. You have a responsibility in your recovery. It appears Ebed-melech did everything, but check out the passage again. Ebed-melech says, *"Put the rags and clothes between your armpits and the ropes."* It does not end there. The next three words are, *"Jeremiah did so."* Jeremiah could not do it alone, but he also could not just sit there pouting expecting someone else to do everything for him. He had to do something. You, too, have a responsibility. God will not stop you from using. He wants you to make that choice. See who God has sent and be willing to work together. There are actions you need to take to help in your recovery.

3. God can use anyone and anything to bring victory. It is intentional that God had him use *"old rags and worn-out clothes."* He could have used new items. He could have been less specific saying they used clothes, but he chose to point out they were *"old and worn-out."* God does not give up on people. He uses the *"old and worn-out"* to make a difference in the world. God can make you a new creation. He gives life.

David understands Jeremiah's rescue and your situation when in Psalm 40:2 he says, *"He drew me up from the pit of destruction, out of the miry bog, and set my feet upon a rock, making my steps secure."* The goal of this book is to help you recover from your mess. You can't do it, but it can be done. It seems it is impossible. Humanly speaking it is a dead end. Only Jesus brings eternal life and life to the full. Only Jesus brings recovery. Give your life to Jesus. As a child of God, when you see the word impossible, you should read it as I-M-possible.

Who has God sent to help you?

_____

_____

_____

_____

What things do you need to do to help in your recovery?

_____

_____

_____

_____

_____

How can God use you to do something special right now?

_____

_____

_____

_____

_____

_____

_____

_____

_____

OUR MISSION

Matthew 28:19-20: *"Go therefore and make disciples of all nations, baptizing them in the name of the Father and of the Son and of the Holy Spirit, teaching them to observe all that I have commanded you. And behold, I am with you always, to the end of the age."*

REACH

At The River Church, you will often hear the phrase, "we don't go to church, we are the Church." We believe that as God's people, our primary purpose and goal is to go out and make disciples of Jesus Christ. We encourage you to reach the world in your local communities.

GATHER

Weekend Gatherings at The River Church are all about Jesus, through singing, giving, serving, baptizing, taking the Lord's Supper, and participating in messages that are all about Jesus and bringing glory to Him. We know that when followers of Christ gather together in unity, it's not only a refresher it's bringing life-change.

GROW

Our Growth Communities are designed to mirror the early church in Acts as having "all things in common." They are smaller collections of believers who spend time together studying the word, knowing and caring for one another relationally, and learning to increase their commitment to Christ by holding one another accountable.

The River Church
8393 E. Holly Rd. Holly, MI 48442
theriverchurch.cc • info@theriverchurch.cc